PROWESS

THE RIGHTLYND SAGA

Rightlynd

Exit Strategy

Sender

Prowess

The Wolf at the End of the Block

Red Rex

Lottery Day

PROWESS

⊱ A PLAY ⊰

IKE HOLTER

NORTHWESTERN UNIVERSITY PRESS
EVANSTON, ILLINOIS

LIBRARY OF CONGRESS
CATALOGING-IN-PUBLICATION DATA

Names: Holter, Ike, 1985– author. | Holter, Ike, 1985– Rightlynd saga.
Title: Prowess : a play / Ike Holter.
Description: Evanston, Illinois : Northwestern University Press, 2019. | Series: Rightlynd saga | "Prowess, by Ike Holter, was originally produced by Jackalope Theatre Company in Chicago, where it ran from November 4 through December 12, 2015. It was directed by Marti Lyons."
Identifiers: LCCN 2019022958 | ISBN 9780810140974 (trade paperback) | ISBN 9780810140967 (ebook)
Subjects: LCSH: Chicago (Ill.)—Drama.
Classification: LCC PS3608.O49435985 P76 2019 | DDC 812/.6—dc23
LC record available at https://lccn.loc.gov/2019022958

CONTENTS

Production History *vii*

Prowess 1

PRODUCTION HISTORY

Prowess, by Ike Holter, was originally produced by Jackalope Theatre Company in Chicago, where it ran from November 4 through December 12, 2015. It was directed by Marti Lyons. Scenic design was by Courtney O'Neill, lighting design by Michael Stanfill, and costume design by Samantha Jones. Matthew Chapman handled the sound design. Corinne Bass was the props director. Oliver Sawa was the dramaturg and Ryan Borque was the fight choreographer, with Alex Hutson as technical director, Danielle Stack as production manager, William Herbet Kiley and Linda Sherfick as assistant directors, and Becky Bishop as stage manager. The cast was as follows:

Jax . . . . Donovan Diaz
Mark . . . . Julian Parker
Zora. . . . . Sydney Charles
Andy . . . . Andrew Goetten/Andrew Burden Swanson

PROWESS

CHARACTERS

Jax. Latinx. Over twenty-five and under forty. Fast-thinking, always self-medicated. Acts like a mix between Catwoman and Banksy. Turns from friend to foe in a split second. Spends most of his time in a very modern superhero costume, complete with a mask that covers most of his face. Uses knives. Wants to do the right thing, but who actually has time for all that?

Mark. About thirty. Black. Built like a brick truck. Band-nerd energy mixed with machismo. A leader. Excellent fighter. Soldier without a war. Uses a billy-bat baton.

Zora. About thirty. Black. Lifelong resident of the Rightlynd neighborhood. Survivor. Goes from mild mannered to ass-kicking militant. Prefers tasers. Got jokes.

Andy. White. Twenty-something. Tech-nerd headcase. Obsessed with comic book crap. Can go from mile-a-minute fast to slow-motion drama. Confuses power with finality. Everybody's best friend. Makes his own instruments of destruction.

NOTE: A slash mark (/) in a character's speech means another character has already started their next line; it's an overlap, and both characters are speaking at the same time. An ellipsis (. . .) in lieu of speech indicates that the characters exchange something silent and necessary. Parenthetical speech means the character is speaking at a (low volume).

SETTING: *Rightlynd*

TIME: *Summer, 2016.*

PROLOGUE

[*Somewhere within the city of Chicago. Pitch black night. A figure cuts in and out of the darkness. His voice comes from everywhere, but we can't see shit.*]

JAX: I'm not sure you're as safe as you think. And that's *not cute,* is
   it? You want to be safe, *need* to be safe, but you're never as safe as
   you think; you lock your doors, close the windows, change your
   passwords, eat right, drink less, pray, when it's worth it you vote,
   don't you, *you vote,* you're a *you're a voter,* right, please, everybody, you're really supposed to vote it's like a thing, *trust me,*
   tried it, and let me tell you, guys: "It's totally safe."
   —You should cover your neck.

[*A train roars overhead . . . the voice resumes, still unseen.*]

   Not sure what you've heard about me, don't know who told you,
   but let's just keep whatever mutual mouth between us shut. I'm
   the one you told yourself you didn't see. I'm the one in between
   the shadows in that absence of light, that sliver of sight, I'm the
   sound of the back door you swore was shut, the reason for the

scream in the dead of night, the streak on top of the skyscraper,
I am—
I'm sorry, I can still taste burrito in my mouth, so sorry, it passed,
don't worry, gone now, skirt steak, so sorry. Where was, *OK OK,*
I'm like *ominous and et cetera*, OK: *don't push me* . . . All you
need to know is that I'm not going anywhere.

[*Suddenly, we see* JAX, *still nothing but a silhouette, dousing a wall
in spray paint as he speaks. We're in an alley. Meanwhile, a low hum
from the distance escalates by the second.*]

. . . Remember what I told you 'bout your neck.

VOLUME 1

ALDERMAN'S OFFICE

[*Night.*]

MARK: Sorry I'm late.

ZORA: Uh—we said, we said ten o'clock, right, it's ten o'clock right
now / so—

MARK: And being on time is not early it's late; you've got a busy life
I've got a busy life and I'm just trying to be respectful and profes-
sional about everybody else's busy life: Nice to meet you, Zora.

ZORA: Nice to meet you, Guy from Craigslist.

MARK: Or, you know, *Mark,* / just Mark—

ZORA: *Mark,* that works, / OK.

MARK: Less formal you know less kinda offical but yeah—

ZORA: I'm sorry about your gym.

MARK: *Their* gym, *that's fine,* they don't want my rental that's fine,
psh, you know, they let anyone with a black belt or a tae kwon do

class do whatever the hell *they let some tae bo guy* with a bachelor's in dance use their classes to teach four nights a week for free—

ZORA: Well he has a degree so—

MARK: OK so moving on, / all right we moving on with this we're moving on—

ZORA: "Moving on," yeah, so, yeah yeah yeah.

MARK: Thank you for contacting me, thank you for letting me in your office, thank you for thinking I'm— Thank you for letting me help you.

ZORA: Who needs a gym, right! (who needs / a—)

MARK: So you wanna start with stretching it out, maybe, / maybe getting a little bit loose.

ZORA: Let's do that, OK, OK let's do that.

MARK: Just get loose, start stretching out, just stretch your / arms like—arms like—

ZORA: Like this, right, just like, arms like / this right—

MARK: Kiiinda like that, yeah, yeah, / that's kinda—

ZORA: "Wooo, look at me, look at me, I'm stretching woo!"

MARK: Know what, OK, let's just skip stretching / OK . . .

ZORA: (It's been a minute / so . . .)

MARK: No problem with that, nothing about that, uh, wanna do some push-ups?

ZORA: Let's do some push-ups.

MARK: Great, awesome, so let's start with that, all right, let's start with twenty push-ups.

ZORA: Twenty—twenty push-ups, OK. OK, let's / do twenty push-ups—

MARK: You wanna listen to like some Beyoncé, some Kendrick, maybe get an underscore / thing going on—

ZORA: Nope! Twenty push-ups in complete silence, let's / just do this!

MARK: All right! . . . This your boss? "Nina Esposito, Alderman of the Fifty-First Ward, fighting for Chicago, fighting for"—*know what*, this poster is uh this poster is really kinda like you / know—

ZORA: I designed it myself.

MARK: This a good poster! / This a real good poster!

ZORA: Thank you.

MARK: So she's one of the good guys or whatever?

ZORA: You saw the commercial.

MARK: Uh-huh.

ZORA: Yeah, so, / what, what—

MARK: I don't know, you know, *just asking* / I guess.

ZORA: So, uh, huge bill, save the city, ohmygod, read a book, / read a paper—

MARK: I saw the commercial.

ZORA: "An alderman set on increasing school protection, keeping the streets clean, saving the neighborhood, and importing unicorns who shit rainbows into / the greater Chicagoland area—"

MARK: I get it. Still tho. I mean that shit she pulled, with the schools, with the cops, I mean a lotta people say—

ZORA: It's complicated and it's rough and I wasn't happy about it either, believe me, but she was in a rough place, and people don't see all sides, just what they wanna see and I think honestly—are you still counting?

MARK: eleven / . . . twelve . . . thirteen . . . fourteen . . . fifteen.

ZORA: (Thank you), uh, I think she's doing something that a lot of people . . . talk about doing but never actually . . . do, *oh wow* this is a lot more intense / than I thought it would be.

MARK: You're doing fine, doing fine, sixteen—

ZORA: I like her. Like her a lot.

MARK: And she pays.

ZORA: *Of course* she pays, / *ohmygod*, of course.

MARK: Not like you're doing this for free / or anything . . .

ZORA: She's an alderman, she's not a prophet or anything, *I get paid*, / don't worry, I get mine.

MARK: You never know, never know.

ZORA: And—that's— / twenty, right?

MARK: That's twenty, nice work, doing OK?

ZORA: Doing great.

MARK: Great, uh—so, you're warm, / right, "are you warm now," like are you together?

ZORA: Oh, I am warmed up, woooo, believe me, push-ups-sit-ups-stand-ups-sit-downs—

MARK: I like to call this Marking It Out . . . You get / it.

ZORA: Oh, I get it, / "ha, I get it."

MARK: You get it! Cause it's my name! / You get it!

ZORA: "I get it."

MARK: OK! Sorry, that was— "Wow, random guy from online is making name jokes," wow (you're not freaked out yet?)—

ZORA: Oh! No, nonono, homie, I got Mace in my desk, / we good, all right.

MARK: Good for you! Good for you!

ZORA: I like to plan ahead, / so let's go.

MARK: Let's keep going, OK, so real quick—before we go any further, uh, I just need to tell you to tell me that if I ever accidently hit you that you won't then sue me. Just a verbal agreement or a handshake or kind of like a head nod or something, just, you know, so it's all *legal*.

ZORA: Oh, that sounds really legal, / actually—

MARK: Fuck, you know what, no, no, that sounds janky as fuck—

ZORA: Mark, if you punch me in the face, I promise that I won't sue your ass, that's my word. Whatever's left of it, there you go, take it.

MARK: SHADAT.

ZORA: . . .

MARK: SHADAT, right, say it with me. / SHADAT, let's start this, OK—

ZORA: "SHADAT," right, SHADAT.

MARK: Sternum, heart, ass, dick, aggressive tactics.

ZORA: Oh that's good, / I like it—

MARK: Thank you, see, most people say nose, eyes, knees, / right?

ZORA: "Who needs 'em?"

MARK: You don't need that stuff, trying to punch someone in the eye is crazyhard, and no offense: but you don't look like Sylvester Stallone.

ZORA: Thank you, it's the hair, / right, it's the hair.

MARK: Don't focus on that, don't focus on that, focus on what's closest to you (stand right there), / yeah right there—

ZORA: Right here?

MARK: What's the first thing in front of you?

ZORA: Your chest.

MARK: Sternum, touch it, tap it, next thing, what else is like *right in front* of you? —Beneath my chest, / beating inside of it—

ZORA: Heart, your heart / your heart, ten points for me on that one.

MARK: There you go, see, right in the middle? That's a kicker, / right?

ZORA: That hurts.

MARK: That hurts, right, but punch someone just *to the right*, punch their heart?

ZORA: OhmyGOD that's / awful—

MARK: They'll be like, "That's some messed up shit, WHAT are you DOING?!" Right?

ZORA: You want me to punch someone in the heart, do people still do that?

MARK: People will always do that, it's like their favorite thing in the / world to do—

ZORA: Should I be taking notes?

MARK: Moving on, all right, the ass, now, very tricky, but it works, right on top of—turn around and grab your ass, please—

ZORA: Really?

MARK: Really really, I'm like a doctor, I take no enjoyment / in this—

ZORA: Got it.

MARK: See now, your ass is the bottom of your back bone and the top priority if you've knocked down your attacker and you're right behind 'em, lift your knee up, BOOM.

ZORA: That's what's up / now, yes, yes!

MARK: "That's what's up, great," now let's talk about dick.

ZORA: Someone has to—

MARK: OH, "Someone has to," / there you go, you funny—

ZORA: "Ohhhhhh!" amiright?!

MARK: All right, now it's a stereotype to hit a guy in the nuts, it hurts, we get it, but, what people don't tell you? VERY hard to do, it's not the big BANG, it's the LITTLE tap to the wang that does the bad business—

ZORA: I'm taking notes—

MARK: Take notes, lightly, see, and this is all about positioning, like "what if you slip, what if you miss"—

ZORA: I might accidently hit his ass-bone.

MARK: You might *mess up*, but using your hand, in a straight line, elbow / aligned, see?

ZORA: Like this—

MARK: Like that, doing that, with extreme force in a focused direction between (I don't know) zero to nine inches below the / waistline of an attacker—

ZORA: I'm getting SOMETHING.

MARK: You're gonna get SOMETHING, right, / you gotta get SOME-THING outta that.

ZORA: So it distracts them.

MARK: Yes, YES, see, all these things—are about distraction.

ZORA: So you can run away. Basically.

MARK: It's actually a crucial / step to—

ZORA: None of that, enough of that, over that. Teach me how to fuck-
ing fight.
—Please.
Sorry, / shit.

MARK: It's fine.

ZORA: No, no, no, you know what: I'm not sorry.

MARK: Also fine.

ZORA: I'm not sorry; I could be out, uh, getting lessons in, in karate
and capoeira and, and Matrix shit, OK, / I could be out—

MARK: Nothing's stopping you.

ZORA: I'M POOR. That's stopping me. And ADR, you seem really
goddamn desperate.

MARK: I'm not / desperate.

ZORA: How many other clients you got?

MARK: I got one.

ZORA: Besides me?

MARK: Damnit *you're good.*

ZORA: *You're desperate,* see, same with me, therefore, we are compati-
ble, so, I want to learn how / to fight.

MARK: No, see, you *think you do—*

ZORA: *I know* I do I don't just / *think.*

MARK: Everybody says that, but when shit gets real nobody really wants to fight back.

ZORA: You've done it.

MARK: Which is why I don't need to go chasing that shit, *I know* what it's like to get hit and once you know . . . Look, I don't want you to—I don't want you to go and follow me down some kind of crazy dark road / of—

ZORA: Uh, what *dark road*?

MARK: I didn't say it like / that! Didn't say it like that.

ZORA: *Yes you did*: "Dark Road" / what the fuck, please—

MARK: Uh, I don't know, OK, uh . . . I don't know, last night I broke up a fight on the train and got hit so hard that I can still hear a ringing inside of my head, that's not a good thing, I don't know. Last week I chased down some pickpocket and when I tried to turn back in all the shit he stole, people thought I was the one who took it in the first place, tried to kick my ass, then I had to fight the people I was trying to help, that's some shit, OK, that's some—I don't know, that seems like some kind of dark dark road . . . I wear this jacket three hundred and sixty-five, twenty-four seven, I only work security like four times a week but I wear it to let people know that whenever you see me, no matter what time, you see Mark and you know that he is always, always always on the clock.

ZORA: You wear it every / day—

MARK: No matter what.

ZORA: That's great.

MARK: Thank you.

ZORA: When you wash it tho?

MARK: Like, like, like a couple / times a—

ZORA: You don't even wash that shit, do / you?

MARK: Yeah I do tho / I wash it sometimes I do . . .

ZORA: (Nah you don't even wash that / shit.)

MARK: Fuck's up with you?

ZORA: . . .

MARK: Look, origin stories are the most important part of this, it's important to remember the reason why we wanna help ourselves, defend ourselves . . .

ZORA: OK then, you go first.

MARK: Uh, I don't need to learn, OK, I am the teacher not the student, *I already know.*

ZORA: Fine, all right, how 'bout I live in a neighborhood that's maybe, oh, four bad things away from becoming a goddamn war zone, how's / that.

MARK: Oh that's real good for Spike Lee but this ain't Chi-Raq girl so I don't buy it, / try again.

ZORA: Fuck you man it is *June twelfth* and it is hot and there are sirens stopping me from sleeping four nights a week. Three Lord Gang . . .

MARK: Just a bunch of dumb-ass kids, they're not about to / do nothing.

ZORA: Last week they beat up some old man in broad daylight, *there are sirens* four nights a week stopping me from sleeping, *shit is 'bout to hit the fan real hard* down here and *you know / it—*

MARK: There's shit everywhere and we've had a bad few months but everybody has, so what, *it'll pass* and when it's gone you'll still feel scared and you'll still feel hard and you'll still wanna fight and until *you tell me why* then I won't know how to give you the skills you need to feel confident and this'll basically just turn into some night class you coulda jumped into at the athletic club 'cause at the end of all this—

ZORA: I am the Girl from the Red Line Train.
—If that makes any difference.

MARK AND ZORA: . . .

ZORA: Twenty-one months. I haven't gone anywhere near a train, because of that, twenty-one months, I can't. And I hate it. I really, really hate / that.

MARK: I'm sorry—

ZORA: Done with that, over that, enough with all that, if you're so sorry then prove it, show it, *teach me how to fight.*

MARK: I'll teach you how to *defend.* Teach you how to evade. Shit I learned on my own, shit I perfected myself, all that, you want it, I got it, it's yours, but if you want someone to take that pain and that poison that you got, if you want me to take it out of you and put it back in someone else then that's on you, miss me on that, not my way, *I am not the one.*
. . . I can help you survive.
Not much, but that's enough.

MARK AND ZORA: . . .

ZORA: "SHADAT."

MARK: "SHADAT."

ZORA: "SHADAT." Game on mafucker let's go!

MARK: What?!

ZORA: Sorry, too soon / with that?

MARK: Way too soon / with all that!

ZORA: My bad, my bad, OK, uh, "Please, let us begin this education and empowerment thing, I am so respectfully excited."

MARK: . . . Game on mafucker let's go.

STREET CORNER

[*That night.* JAX *spray paints.* MARK *passes by holding a case of beer.*]

MARK AND JAX: . . .

JAX: Take a picture, it'll last longer . . . Literally. Street cleaners nab
    this stuff by morning, so come on, take a pic, chop chop.

MARK [*reading the graffiti*]: O.M.F.G.

JAX: Hash-tag me, I'll find it, make sure you get the full body, I'll crop
    it later.

MARK: That's, / that's—

JAX: That's my tag, you've seen it around,
    my name, you've heard it somewhere,
    my art, once again,
    thank you for your attendance.

MARK: Do you want some feedback?

JAX [*looking at him for the first time*]: . . . This bitch.

MARK: Cool, 'cause from where I'm standing, I'm a little confused,
    uh—well, first of all, let's start with the color; very poppy, very

comic-booky, I like the flavor, and the message, wow, real deep stuff here man. But right now we have a man under a mask who's ruining a perfectly good building by spray painting on the side of it. Nice attempt, but presentation is everything. Just my opinion.

JAX: . . . Actually. Know what?

MARK: What.

JAX: Thank you, thank you / for that.

MARK: No problem, happy to help.

JAX: You remind me of my favorite art teacher in high school.

MARK: Awww . . .

JAX: I set her classroom on fire and took a dump on her Nissan; / uncanny resemblance . . .

MARK: Hey, man, look—

JAX: "Hey, man, / look—"

MARK: Not here to start anything, I'm just saying, / all right.

JAX: "Just saying, all right."

MARK: Look at you, so witty, the jokes just / keep coming.

JAX: Know what, you look so familiar to me, I'm sorry, but are you one of the Wayans brothers?

MARK: Wow.

JAX: Shawn Marlon Lagunitas Wayans, what's your IMDb, who are you?

MARK: Least I'm looking out for my neighborhood.

JAX: You put out the ad. That's you, isn't it, you put out the ad, online, trying to teach people self-defense, you put out the ad, that is *so cute.*

MARK: Nuh-uh, / man.

JAX: That's not you?

MARK: Not like / that, no, so, psssh, like—

JAX: *Looks like you*, looks a lot like you, Rin Tin Light Skin, oh yeah that's you.

MARK: Yeah, but *it's not cute tho,* / it's it's—

JAX: Oh, it's cute.

MARK: No, it's not cute, it's fucking like, like masculine and stuff.

JAX: (Oh honey / no honey, no.)

MARK: So. Yeah. So, nah mean, yeah, what, son, / yeah . . .

JAX: Whatthefuck.

MARK: Nevermind, OK, *see you don't even get it man,* you're running around tearing up this place like some Dollar Store Banksy, I'm fucking trying to pull people together, I'm trying to save this place, I'm trying to do something good.

JAX: Someone shot a five-year-old yesterday two feet from where you're standing. Try harder.
Drive-by. Think they were aiming for someone else, but you know you never can tell around Rightlynd, can you. O.M.F.G. *I do this for her,* and him, and the nameless them and I won't stop, because this doesn't stop and tonight it'll be something else, and I'll spray, then again tomorrow, and I'll spray, and after the ambulances wash that away *and that away* and every speck of blood seeps into concrete so we forget, I will always, always be there to remind us that *we cannot, I do this for them.*
—Now I don't know what paticulaur brand of faggotry you're attempting. But for the love of God take down that shit on Craigslist, it is mamby-pamby bullshit and it is pathetic, see, you are a Band-Aid on an infection bubbling yellow with oozing

puss; I'm a free ride to the hospital with a really good soundtrack; *let me work.*

MARK: Step away from that wall.

JAX: "Step away from that / wall."

MARK: Dude. Look. If I were you—

JAX: You'd have the upper hand in this situation.

MARK: If I were you, I would get the fuck out of this place or else.

JAX: Or else what?

[JAX *reaches into* MARK's *bag. Pulls out a beer. Opens it. What a bitch.*]

Actions speak louder than words but your silence is oddly sonic; surround sound, keep it down, you'll wake the neighbors. High Life? This neighborhood really is circling the flush, good luck.

[JAX *throws the beer on the ground.*]

MARK: . . . That's it?

JAX: "That's it," yes, what, you thought—

MARK: I thought, I don't know, I thought we fight—

JAX: And then you'd win.

MARK: But then you'd get away like right at the last minute, / like—

JAX: All like, "I'll get you next time / motherfucker!"

MARK: Haha yeah I thought this would be *like a thing* / you know . . .

JAX: Franchise potential, all that / uh-huh.

MARK: Thought it would be a thing.

JAX: Not a thing, nice to meet / you, hi—

MARK: Mark, hi, are / we shaking hands now?

JAX: We are shaking hands now, yes, / hi, ohmygod.

MARK: Weird, right, uh Mr. O.M.F.G., / yeah?

JAX: What, no, what, code names are infantile, no—Jax— / hello, how are you?

MARK: Jax, nice knowing you, been fun, thanks for the chat and— good luck.

JAX: —*mmmnnnn* that seems . . . a little bit presumptuous, don't / you think?

MARK: Nope, seems just right, you have a good life / man!

JAX: To Be Continued!

MARK: The End.

JAX: Nuh-huh.

MARK: Yeah-huh.

JAX: ACT TWO!

MARK: END SCENE CURTAIN CLOSE, No Sequel For You: / Bye now!

JAX: Yeah there will be lots of sequels tho, for me, nevermind piss off EAT A DICK FUCK FAIRY.

[MARK *is gone.* JAX *basically turns to the audience.*]

I hate feedback . . . before you're finished.

ALDERMAN'S OFFICE

[ZORA *and* MARK. *Week later.*]

MARK: One more time?

ZORA: Fifty more times, a hundred more times, / let's go.

MARK: Couple more times, now as soon as I / put my hand up.

ZORA: Five hits in ten seconds as soon as you put your hand up.

MARK: Which is hard—

ZORA: I got this.

MARK: You've got this but it's also hard, / we'll try again.

ZORA: Serve it up bring it on lemme have it I'm ready.

MARK: OK. So this time I won't go easy on you.

ZORA: "Oh, shit."

MARK: Focus.

ZORA AND MARK: . . .

MARK: Now.

[MARK *raises his hand;* ZORA *punches it twice, moving with him, until* MARK *grabs her, throws her against the cabinets.*]

MARK: Two out of five, / you're *learning*, you're totally learning—

ZORA: Ohmygod why the fuck are you so fast—

MARK: Two out of five, better than last time.

ZORA: What's the secret?

MARK: There is no secret.

ZORA: There is totally a secret, you're doing some up-down, up-down, A-B start bullshit and you / need to tell me the secret—

MARK: You're standing wrong. FOCUS, you're standing wrong. When you stand like this you're a brick, when you stand like that, I can knock you over / in like three seconds.

ZORA: Like this, like this, / right, right?

MARK: That's it, you got it—

ZORA: I got it—

MARK: One more time.

ZORA: Seventy more times, / I've got it, I've got it, let's go.

MARK: *Uh no, no, one more time,* focus IN five, four, three, two—

ANDY [*entering*]: Holy shit.

MARK: Uhhhhhhh / hhhhhhhhhhhhhhhhh.

ZORA: No, nonononono. Andy, what the fuck??

ANDY: I forgot my / my my my thing, in the office, my thing, I'm sorry, I'm sorry, OK, I'M SORRY.

ZORA: This office is closed, it closes at six and it's eight-thirty now and it's closed, OK, CLOSED!

EVERYONE: . . .

ANDY: So I'm gonna go get that / thing.

ZORA: Go get your thing.

ANDY: So sorry, so sorry.

ZORA AND MARK: . . .

MARK: (hahahahahahaha)

ZORA: This is not hilarious.

MARK: You're totally right.

ZORA: (Ohmygod.)

MARK: Sorry 'bout that.

ZORA: (Ohmygod.)

EVERYONE: . . .

ANDY: Got it.

ZORA: Good.

ANDY: Just a zip drive.

ZORA: A zip drive.

ANDY: But I got it now, / so—

ZORA: That's great.

ANDY: Got the zip drive, gonna zip out, / so—

ZORA: So good night, Andy, good night.

ANDY: New site tomorrow, / too—

ZORA: YES.

ANDY: Kind of excited about it.

ZORA: I am too.

ANDY: Really?

ZORA: Fuck no, Andy, nuh-uh, no, bye-bye now.

ANDY: OK.

EVERYONE: . . .

ANDY: But I just have one more / question—

ZORA: Who the fuck dropped you however long ago and now left this shit for us / to deal with?

ANDY: Zora, the question . . . is not for you . . . You're the guy from Craigslist.

MARK: Uh—

ANDY: The self-defense guy, the SHADAT guy, the awesome awesome awesome guy.

MARK: . . . I'm the guy from Craigslist.

ZORA: Ohmygod / why did you answer him, don't ANSWER him, ohmygod . . .

ANDY: Yes, yes, YES, I know you were real, I totally knew it, you must be training like a shitload of people.

MARK: Just one.

ANDY: Just one?

ZORA: Just me.

MARK: But it's fine, I don't care if it's two people or two hundred, it's worth it.

ANDY: *What if it's three?*

MARK: Right, whether it's three or three hundred, / it's worth it—

ANDY: Not three hundred, I meant Zora, you, and me. Three of us, does that does that work, is that is that / possible?

ZORA: No, no, no, / no, nononononono.

ANDY: Here's what I'm thinking (bear with me), here's what I'm thinking . . .

MARK: So he's like / a—

ZORA: The office busybody, he's a NARC.

ANDY: I am not / a narc—

ZORA: Who told Nina I took that pencil sharpener?

ANDY: Well I do believe in some kind of higher order.

ZORA: PENCIL SHARPENER.

ANDY: You've been coming in the last ten days busted, covered in bruises, and I never even said ANYTHING to anybody about your constant case of black eye which you apparently get from doing awesome Kung Fu Matrix Shit. Just one test drive, try me out, I'm super tough, it'll be fast too, uh, we can do like a Training Montage or something, / right, like a—

MARK: *No training montage, /* ever, ever, that is NOT something that actually happens—

ZORA: You just wanna stir the pot, don't you, / just stir it up.

ANDY: Well, what do you want then, I'M IN, andandand I need this from you, so what do you need from me?

MARK: Andy, gimme something!

ANDY: . . . Like, OH, do you want like twenty bucks, do you want like money or something? / I can do that—

ZORA: RACIST.

ANDY: NOT RACIST.

MARK: ANDY. I don't need money. Not doing this for cash, OK, I made this thing so I can fix something that was broken.

ANDY: Oh I am all about that, fuck yeah.

MARK: Too thirsty.

ANDY: So sorry.

MARK: But *you feel me*, all right, that's my thing, now Zora over here—

ANDY: Is the Girl from the Red Line Train.

ZORA: You call me that one / more time—

MARK: That's why she's here, it's personal, now you—

ANDY: Have reasons.

ZORA: Fuck you do.

ANDY: You know I'm not being rude here, but Zora, whatever happened to you happens to a lot of us.

ZORA: . . .

MARK: Andy—

ZORA: *Not like that,*
    not to you,
    it doesn't, it can't, and it never fucking will.
    It never fucking will,
    Not Like That.

ANDY: . . . You're right. I'm. I'm sorry, / I'm sorry—

ZORA: Say that shit again.

ANDY: I'm sorry, I'm sorry, OK, and, and I'll go, / OK—

ZORA: Thank you very much.

ANDY: 'Cause everybody's pain, right, everybody else's pain always,
 always wins. I'm just a (fuck), right, I mean, I'm just some white
 boy, right, nothing bad can ever really happen to me, right, last
 year my—
 Last year, my two best friends in the world went into a gas station.
 And some—guys, I don't know, some guys—
 Held them up. Everyone in the store. Four people.
 Said they'd let 'em go, soon as it was done,
 "in and out." I heard that from the car, "in and out," I heard that . . .
 So they took their money.
 Cellphones, credit cards, wallets, and . . . Took it all.

ZORA: Well, OK, "ohmygod," fine, I'm sorry—

ANDY: And then they shot them.
 Four people.
 Just shot them all, one by one,
 right down the line, my two best friends,
 trapped in there, trapped in there and just bam, bam, bam, bam,
 BAM, bambambambambam.
 . . . And they left.
 And I was in the car.
 And they walked right past me.
 And I and I, I, I just slid down in the seat, so they wouldn't see me.
 Never caught, never caught, no, gone,
 my two best friends, in the world, two bullets in their heads dead,
 gone, just—
 . . . Still. Not as bad as "The Girl on the Red Line Train."
 No. Your pain? Your pain always wins.

MARK: . . . I need to know that you're serious.

ANDY: What—what, what, were you were you listening, / COME ON, fuck, I am totally serious.

ZORA: Andy, not like that, what he's saying / is—

ANDY [*open heart*]: I'm serious, everybody knows that, I'm totally serious, I, I, I, I was top of my class at Northwestern and I'm obsessed with getting things right and this is my seventh (sorry) EIGHTH job in the last year because I can't focus on anything because I don't have any friends anymore and I don't have a life anymore and I wake up every morning with this deep deep pit of shame and regret and anger so much anger, so much anger inside of me, and my therapist told me to channel it so just point me in the right direction, I have lightning electricity waiting to jump out of me like a rat in a trashcan, just gimme something, trust that something will *be* something, give me anything, Jesus Christ: everybody says I'm so serious *that it's sad.*

EVERYONE: . . .

MARK: If we do this: you never say the words "training montage" in my presence / again.

ANDY: (*Not even in a / whisper.*)

MARK: Never again.

ANDY: Deal.

MARK: Jump in—

ANDY: OK.

MARK: This is called Backhand: I raise my hand, as soon as I do that you try to get five hits into my forearms in ten seconds, you'll fail at first but then you'll get halfway there in no time—

ANDY: OK, right off the bat, you should probably know that I've never hit anyone.

MARK: I figured that out already. / We'll start slow, we'll start easy, we have time; it's fine—

ANDY: Just thought I should let you know because you know, because it's just, it's just, uh, I'm just a little—OK. No, no, OK, I'm ready, "Backhand," let's do this.

ZORA: . . . Andy. Move your legs. It's about how you stand; focus, you stand like that he'll knock you down, stand like this, you're a brick, OK, you're a brick.

ANDY: I've always wanted to be a brick.

EVERYONE: . . .

MARK: Five, four, three, two . . .

STOOP

[*Two weeks later. Night.* ANDY *is in like bad shape. He tries to roll a joint.*]

ANDY: Ow. Ow ow ow. Ow ow ow. Fuck me ow . . . OK. OK. No, OK (here it is again), ow ow ow, fuck me, ow—

[*A car slow rolls by.* ANDY *watches it for a second—looks away. He doesn't breathe, he doesn't move, he's terrified. It idles . . . then speeds off.* ANDY *catches his breath, gasping.* ZORA *approaches with a bag; hydrogen peroxide and Band-Aids and shit. She sits him down on the stoop and fixes his shit.*]

ZORA: How you holding up?

ANDY: Oh man I'm I'm I'm OK, I guess, like I—you know, I mean "*pshhh,*" whatever, / man, I'm fine, "I'm good, I AM WELL."

ZORA: There you go, see, see, YEAH boy there you go.
    —Who was in that car?

ANDY: I don't, uh, I don't / know.

ZORA: So why were you looking at that car?

ANDY: I tried / not—

ZORA: Don't try, next time you see a slow roll come by *you try nothing*. Three Lord Gang—

ANDY: I know fucking Three / Lord Gang.

ZORA: Then act like it. They're spreading real quick and when they come by you turn your head to the side, when they come around *you do not exist.*

ANDY: If I could be invisible, I would be invisible, but I can't, so I'm just I'm just I'm—I'm *trying.* Been here for eight months. I'm trying. My neighbor saw me move in, and she looked at me and she said, "Wow, look at you, I bet there's finna be a Starbucks on the corner in six months," but it's been eight months now so where / is the Starbucks on the corner?!

ZORA: Hahahahahahaha, hahahaha, you *can't even gentrify correctly* / can you?!

ANDY: I am trying to gentrify the fuck out of this place but it isn't working! How long before they stop, like—how long / before—

ZORA: How long before everybody stops looking at you like you don't belong here, *I hope never, bitch,* I pray for progress, / OK.

ANDY: "I hurt sooooooooooooo / muuuuuuuch."

ZORA: "Yes let the white tears flow to the streets," gimme your hand—

ANDY: Please be dainty.

ZORA: Gimme your hand, it's gonna be fine, how bad can it—WHOA / OK, OK—

ANDY: Icky, right, that's gross, / right—

ZORA: OKOKOK, uh—I got this, I got this, gimme two minutes, I got this, and tomorrow if Nina asks you anything—

ANDY: Nina doesn't even look me in the eye, she's like Tom Cruise, only taller and less awesome, OW—

ZORA: Sorry.

ANDY: I mean "oh, whatever," / you know—

ZORA: There you go, keep bullshiting, but no, for real, all right, precautionary measures here. If she asks anything—say you play rugby.

ANDY: Uh—

ZORA: Well you can't say badminton 'cause that's what I've been telling her.

ANDY: Badminton?

ZORA: Badminton's mine, get something / else.

ANDY: BADMINTON.

ZORA: Well yeah, after you punched me last time, / uh, YEAH—

ANDY: Uh, too bad, we were working on ducking, *you were supposed / to duck.*

ZORA: Well, shit happens, OK, and now my boss thinks that I'm just really bad at badminton instead of being really awesome at getting my ass kicked.

ANDY: She's screwed.

ZORA: She's gonna / be fine.

ANDY: People-hate-her, and people could vote her out, 'cause this neighborhood is just out of fucking control, *but no*, no, nobody gets out, nobody cares, know what I think? I think maybe we should just start telling her what goes on there after hours, you know, maybe people would endorse someone who believes people need to defend themselves instead of waiting on a system that takes six months to put up a stop sign, I think maybe then people would vote for an alderman who can actually get stuff done instead of just letting things pass and kissing the mayor's ass, OW—

ZORA: Damn right "ow," don't say that shit, she's trying, all right?

ANDY: Well she's really blowing at it / tho—

ZORA: OK, so what are you doing, then, huh what / you got?

ANDY: Uh.

ZORA: That's right, you ain't got shit, so you just complain about someone else trying to do something 'cause you're too fucking lazy to do anything in the first place. You wanna change something, then change it, what the fuck is stopping you?

ANDY: Well what the fuck is stopping you?! . . . Sorry, was that too hardcore, sometimes I get too hardcore—I'm sorry, I'm not hardcore.

ZORA: She's almost there, k? She's slow to take up some causes, still getting her footing right, but it's not easy being alderman, k, real tough job, out here, right now, so I'll stick with it till shit starts to fall off; close your fingers—

ANDY: Fingers closed.

ZORA: Relax your hand.

ANDY: Hand relaxed as fuck, *oh my god thank / you—*

ZORA: And if anybody asks tomorrow you're / gonna say—

ANDY: I'm gonna say I play rugby.

ZORA: Why?

ANDY AND ZORA: " 'Cause nobody asks follow-up questions if you say you play rugby."

ANDY: God / you suck, you fucking suck—

ZORA: "Ohhhhhh better, now baby, / are you better?"

ANDY: It doesn't even hurt, whatever, I'm fine.

ZORA: "He's better," now look, ice, take it, take the whole bag home, you think it's fine now, wait until the morning, keep treating it / till it's treated.

ANDY: I'm not taking this whole bag, / come on.

ZORA: It's like four bucks of stuff, / you need it, honey.

ANDY: I saw you hit the ground, hard, there's probably scars all over your back, come on, I've got a million drugs and bottles and Band-Aids at home, here, take it—

ZORA [*real big sister shit*]: Only one of us can walk into a convenience store without getting flashbacks and loss of breath and that one of us is not you. OK? Andy? OK? . . . Take the goddamn bag. —We good?

ANDY: We good.

JAX: Well I prefer Vicodin but then again I'm not a pussy.

[JAX *suddenly appears, hanging off the streetlight. He crosses.*]

. . . Hello, they call me Jax, I'm mentally unstable and I've been stalking you, please don't be alarmed.

ANDY: . . . Hey, my name's Andy and this is my apartment / so—

ZORA: (Stop fucking speaking.)

ANDY: OK nevermind, / so sorry.

ZORA: Look, why don't you go on and have a good night, man, all right? Not looking for—well, whatever the fuck you got, frankly, 'cause there's a lot of *stuff happening here*, OK, and whatever it is, we don't need it, so please keep it: "Have a good night, man, all right."

JAX: That's where I know you from. The *Tribune*. Two years back, you—are the Girl from the Red Line Train.

ZORA: I said have a good night / man, all right—

JAX: The Girl from the Red Line Train, wow wow WOW. And where are you from?

ANDY: Schaumburg.

JAX: You both have such tragic stories, wow wow wow—

ZORA: You should leave—

JAX: And you should shut your face. I said shut your fucking face Azealia Banks, SHUT IT . . . Bartholomew. Bartholomew. Hello, hello, I'm talking to you, / kid, hello—

ANDY: My name's Andy, / actually—

JAX: *You look* like a fucking Bartholomew. Question, kid: Who did that to your arm?

ZORA: Shut up, Andy.

JAX: I see all this shit. Every block, every house, every ho down in hellville, I *know how this clock ticks* . . . and five nights a week I see three people exit the alderman's office limping, now, who did that your arm? Was it Lenny Kravitz with the Members Only jacket, because if so then I have hit the jackpot, honey. Now, I will find this out the hard way if the easy way seems too difficult . . . So, please tell me what the hell is happening with Lenny fucking Kravitz in the Members Only jacket?

ANDY: We train—

JAX: For what?

ANDY: Self-defense.

JAX: No fighting?

ANDY: No fighting.

JAX: *No fighting,* no "parry parry, / thrust thrust"—

ANDY: We're taking it slow.

JAX: Just "get away from me, I know tae bo," no fighting, / *that's it?*

ZORA: For now—

JAX: Know what, there is an *odd tone* coming out of your mouth and I think you're in proper need of a tune-up.

ZORA: Is that / a—

JAX: That is not a threat, that is simply an opportunity for you to be very afraid of what I can do to you.

ZORA: You're assuming I can't handle myself because I'm a woman.

JAX: Bitch, I'm a feminist.

ZORA: Say that to my face.

JAX: Get back in your binder.

ANDY: This sounds like a sit-down conversation.

JAX: NOBODY MOVES now—if what Bartholomew is telling me is true, then you two have been joining forces and stepping it up with SideShow Bob Mocha Choca Latta, now, is that correct, Girl from the Red Line Train, have I hit upon something correct? —I need you to send him a message.

ZORA: I need you / to back the fuck—

JAX: Oh, I see what's happening here. Got your ass handed to you, talk of the city, and now you're trying to pull yourself together with that Dollar Store DJ Jazzy Jeff, I see, I see, word of advice (if I may, OK), honey, he's not snacking on what you're serving, and if I were you I'd save my breath and keep my legs closed—

ZORA [*stepping up to him*]: THE FUCK / YOU SAY TO ME, say that to my face, say that to my face, MOTHERFUCKEEEEEEER!

ANDY: (Zora. We don't have to do this. We don't have to do this, / we don't have to do this, ZORA!)

[ZORA *charges. With one kick,* JAX *knocks her to the other side of the roof.*]

JAX: Now comes time for the question and answer format of our lesson: Zora, how does that feel?

ZORA: (. . . fuck, fuck, / fuck.)

JAX: Incorrect, I believe "ow, ohmygod, ow" was the answer you were looking for, / please pay attention.

ANDY [*trying to help her up*]: OK, OK, we got this, OK, just stay down, / just don't move, stay down.

JAX: Yet again at the mercy of a man who is deciding your fate, Zora, how does that feel, and please speak up so the / whole class can hear you.

ANDY: Come with me, we're gonna run, just stay down—

JAX: Yes, stay down, Zora, stay down, keep where you're better acquainted—

[ZORA *rushes at* JAX. *PUNCH, KICK, PUNCH, no direct hits.* JAX *lights a cigarette as he knees her in the stomach, grabs her hair, and throws her to the ground. She falls like a stack of bricks.*]

. . . Next?

ANDY: Just leave us alone, please, please, just just leave us alone, / you you you got what you wanted, please—

JAX: "Please, please, please," ohmygod just stop your begging, do you realize what you're doing, you're a white twenty-something with a nice job, passable style, the whole world ahead of you, but look at yourself, you're begging, your people don't beg. That pleasure is reserved for the lesser of our species, that pleasure is for people like me.

[JAX *grabs* ANDY *by the hair.*]

Hit me. Hit me. Come on, hit me, / five, four, three, two, one—

ANDY: Wait, please-please-please—

JAX: Andy, you have immense power that goes untapped and bottled like a keg without the cap, you, my friend, are a waste to your race and I am sorry to say that you have failed this lesson.

[JAX *punches* ANDY. *Once, twice, three times in the chest.* ANDY *falls to the ground.* ZORA *and* ANDY *lie there, exhausted, weak, useless.* JAX *reaches into his pocket and approaches.*]

JAX: I like *totally fear for this city. Like MAN.* Man. I am like *fearful and stuff.*
You two wanna change things? You can't change shit, just hunker down, look around, this is your town, this is it. *Don't like it, move,* love it, stay, but *adapt, see—*
Kicking someone in the shins and showing real moxie won't do shit when the other person actually has a gun and, spoiler alert, but the other person always, always has a gun, so RUN.
Do not fight back. When someone comes, you go; you are not strong, you are not super, *you are nothing.*

. . . And it's my job to make sure that's something you never forget.

[JAX *takes out whatever's in his pocket. They scream.*]

VOLUME 2

ALDERMAN'S OFFICE

[*That night. We see* MARK. *He has medical supplies.* ANDY *is on the ground, face down.*]

MARK: In . . . and out . . . just in . . . and out, / keep doing it, keep doing it—

ANDY: (It hurts. So. Much.)

MARK: I know it does, I know it does, just keep breathing, OK? Just in, and out, and in, and out, there you go, there you go . . . Zora? Are you OK to come out here or do you need / more—

ZORA: I'm fine.

MARK: OK . . . We can actually start fixing this if you come out here, / so—

ZORA: GIVE ME A SECOND.

MARK: Just come out here. And show me what he did. Can you take your hand off your forehead? Please?

[*She does. Written in large black Sharpie is the word LOSER.*]

MARK: Oh!

ZORA: "Oh, / oh," yeah, yeah, "OH."

MARK: OH, "sorry," oh, OH, what the fuck?

ZORA: Oh yeah.

MARK: What the / fuck, really? Really?

ZORA: Yeah, uh, he gave us this huge speech—

ANDY: More of a soliloquy.

ZORA: And then he beat the shit out of us and he wrote this on my forehead.

ANDY: He pressed down really, really hard.

[ANDY *sits up. The words BUTT PLUG are sharpied on his forehead.*]

I mean: that's a little excessive. Right? It's not just me, / right, THANK you.

MARK: (hahahaha) No that's really fucked up, / man, for real fucked up—

ZORA: *Why you laughing / I see you laughing.*

MARK: *I'm / not even laughing.*

ZORA: Yeah, you got the giggles right now, you laughing, *what's funny / about this, Mark?*

MARK: Uh, *what's funny* is that I told you guys to not stir shit up and here you go, stirring shit up, right, and I know what's up, OK, you both walk around like I'm holding you down but soon as you try to jump in you get knocked down, proving me right, so I am

RIGHT right now and that, that's pretty funny to me, right now, I am *amused*.

ANDY: He knows where I live.

MARK: He's harmless, he's an artist, he's just weird and lost and desperate, he's fucking stupid . . . Did he say anything about me, tho?

ANDY: Uh no, not, / not really, not to my knowledge, no.

MARK: Really? All right, cool, OK, I mean whatever, / I mean—

ZORA: DONT PLAY, NIGGA, DONT / PLAY.

MARK: Just wondering, doesn't matter, hey: next time you see him, you run, it's not funny, it's not cute, you are lucky to be breathing / right now.

ZORA: He's lucky, / I—

MARK: Nuh-uh-uh you do NOT step to me, not tonight, do NOT . . . You messed up. You admit that. Or this all stops right here, right now, you admit that you fucked the fuck up and now you need me, you admit that.

ZORA: . . . We are not admitting anything / to you.

ANDY: We fucked the fuck up, and I am so sorry, man, I am so / so sorry.

MARK: Thank you, Andy.

ANDY: I'm so sorry, I'm so, so sorry.

MARK: Go wash up.

ANDY: I tried, I, I I tried to be a brick / OK I—

MARK: Just Go.

[ANDY *leaves.*]

ZORA: . . . I'm still scared of the train. Twenty-two months later, everytime it goes by, I—I hide *inside* myself, and it makes me weak, k, you wanna hear that, there you go, I feel weak. You were supposed to make me strong but all I feel is weak.

MARK: We're taking it slow.

ZORA: I coulda died tonight, fuck *slow.*
—When I charged those mafuckers on the train? News said there were two, three.
No. There were five.
Late night, picking on some girl, just fucking with her, some girl, looking just like me, "out at night where she shouldn't be," on the train, on the goddamn train, seen it happen time and time again but that night, fuck it.
Coulda been me. Fuck *them.*
All I had was a bottle of wine—
Bam, right over the head of the shortest one, I was in heels, stepped straight on the knee of the tallest one, BOOM, climbed him like a goddamn flagpole and didn't stop the hits, didn't stop the hits, even when they found me unconscious bleeding out of my head on the floor of that train, the cops said my hands were still going up and down, up and down, "just-*one-more-hit.*"
—And you're right, Mark, *you are right,* tonight I coulda gotten my throat slit up and Andy should be knocked down dead on the ground, both of us, and I just keep thinking that he's followed us, followed us here, 'bout to pop up and finish the job, just keep thinking, "They're not finished with me yet." *I haven't thought that* since the train and that kept my mind up at night for months, started to go away, now it's back, "They're not finished with me yet." I don't want anybody else ever, ever, ever having the power to keep my mind up at night, so there you go, *I'm sorry.*

[ANDY *enters.*]

I know how to defend.

I know how to react.

And you say that's your limit, and I respect that, Mark, I know all that.

But if he comes back and someone else gets hurt or worse, then you are complicit,

teach us how to fight or *we are dead.*

EVERYONE: . . .

MARK: Three blocks down. My apartment. There's a, there's a roof. Not much. But it's not here.

We can use it for training—

ANDY: What kind of training?

MARK: Tomorrow night. And every night this week till summer's up, no stops, no breaks, we do this, we do this, correct. Both of you. I owe you that . . . Andy?

ANDY: Well, I'm, I'm fully committed and I'm excited / and—

MARK: None of that, please, Andy: say what you need to say.

ANDY: Really?

MARK: Say it.

ANDY: . . . Let's do a motherfucking training montage.

"ACTUALLY AWESOME TRAINING MONTAGE"

[*The title says it all. Scenes start and fall apart, but it all takes place on the roof of* MARK's *apartment. This spans weeks. Hot and sexy tasty jams underscore this entire section.*]

MARK: Aaaaaaaaaaaaaaaaaaaaaaand—punch, block, duck, weave / and, punch, block, duck, weave—

ZORA: "And punch, weave, duck," fuck, FUCK I fucked it up—

ANDY: Is this choreography?

MARK: Start from the top.

ZORA: Got it, got it.

ANDY: How many times do we have to do this?

ZORA AND MARK: Until we get it right!

ANDY: That was *awesome*.

ZORA: I know, / right?

MARK: Again, from the top, GO—

[*Transition.*]

MARK: Knees, shoulders, chest, head,
    pads for everything,
    put 'em on,
    from this point on, we are going into full body contact,
    I don't care if you're angry
    I don't care if you're nervous,
    I don't care if you ate like thirty-five bagels today and feel like
    you're about to throw up,
    all I care about, right now,
    is your safety,
    because from this point on,
    we're going for blood.

ANDY: Sir, yes sir!

MARK: Unnecessary.

ANDY: I mean whatever, man.

MARK: Ready?

ZORA: Ready.

MARK: Ready?

ANDY: Ready!

MARK: FIGHT!

ZORA AND ANDY: . . .

MARK: I'm sorry, maybe, maybe I wasn't clear, uh—
    Zora. Fight Andy.
    Andy. Fight Zora.

ZORA: WHAT.

MARK: Let's go, / come on come on, MOVE!

ZORA: Whoa, whoa whoa, time out, OK, I can't fight him—

MARK: You're-wearing-helmets.

ZORA: Look at him, he's ninety pounds, he barely passed SHADAT, I-will-break-him—

MARK: Zora, / for the last time, no, FOR THE LAST TIME.

ZORA: You're giving us all these rules and then just breaking them, one by one, this-isn't-working, you said we were gonna take it slow, he's still got training wheels and I refuse to / even waste my time on—

ANDY: LOOK WHAT CAME IN THE MAIL!

[ANDY *punches* ZORA *in the face. She falls to the ground. Everything stops.*]

EVERYONE: . . .

ZORA [*in hellish pain*]: Ohmygod I barely felt that.

MARK: She's / good! She's good! She's all good!

ANDY: YES! YES! YES!

ZORA: "She's good! She's good!"

[*Transition.*]

MARK: All right, next scenario:
Zora, you're walking home, it's late, it's dark, it's Pilsen.
Andy, you're a pimp on the lookout for new trade, you're high, you're drunk, you're angry.
GO!

ANDY [*a terrible actor*]: . . . "Hey, what's up, I'm just some guy who wants to make you part of my meat factory, you gonna be my ho fo life, girl, I hope that's OK with you."

MARK: Avoid.

ZORA: "No thanks, I'm too busy being a career girl and killing the game."

MARK: Resist.

ANDY: "Well, I have different opinions about that subject."

MARK: Warn.

ZORA: "I will send you back to hell."

MARK: Bigger warning.

ZORA: "I will send you back to school."

MARK: Final Warning.

ZORA: "I will send you back into your mother's body and take her with me to Planned Parenthood where I will be her support system as she has you ABORTED."

ANDY: "Actually, that really hurts my feelings / so—"

MARK: FIGHT! FIGHT! FIGHT! FIGHT!

[*They fight. It's awesome.* ZORA *wins.* ANDY *drops to the ground, exhausted.*]

ANDY: "So . . . call me?"

ZORA: "I'm usually free most Fridays."

MARK: SCENE!

[*Transition.* ZORA *and* ANDY *move in nearly perfect formation.*]

ZORA: One—

ANDY: Two—

ZORA AND ANDY: / One. Two. Three.

MARK: Aaaaaaaaaaaaaaaaaaaaaaand—punch, block, duck, weave / and, punch, block, duck, weave—

ALL: And, punch, block, duck, weave, and punch, block, duck, weave—

MARK: Now cross it back / and cross it over, up and down, then start all over.

ZORA AND ANDY [completely fucking up]: And cross it, cross and oh fuck, fuck me, fuckfuckfuck damn fuck / Aaaand I got really confident but now I'm lost, now I'm, lost, now I'm lost—

[Transition.]

MARK: Go back to combinations, / come on, getting sloppy, ZORA.

ZORA: Stop NARRATING, / Mark, it's really pissing-me-off.

ANDY: I've got this, / I totally got this, I got it, I got it—

MARK: Head in the game, head in the game—ANDY! Tag me in.

ANDY: Tag me out.

MARK: Zora, / lesson number thirty—

ZORA: No more speeches, no more mantras, / just give-me-a-second!

MARK: When someone comes at you with a / punch to the left, come on—

ZORA: I know, I know, just give-me-a-minute— / Mark, Jesus—

MARK: You're slowing up lately, you're tagging out too much, look at me—

ZORA: I'm taking a five—

MARK: Look at me.

ZORA: FIVE-MINUTE BREAK.

MARK: They didn't give you a five-minute break when you were in the back of that train.

EVERYONE: . . .

MARK: Nobody yelled stop. Nobody tagged out. Didn't get a chance to stop that time.

ZORA: . . .

ANDY: Um . . .

MARK: I tagged you out, Andy, stay quiet . . . You didn't have a chance to yell "break," no time for that, not that time, not that time . . . when they came at / you—

ANDY: (Mark, / man . . . stop . . . I mean it . . . Mark . . . dude . . . No . . . No, no . . . no, no no no . . . MARK, dude, come on man, no. Leave her alone, tag me in, MARK, leave-her-alone. Don't listen, don't listen to him, Mark, MARK—STOP IT—)

MARK: Stay back. Now Zora, when they came at you, I'm sure you did yell, a lot, "Stop," "Game over," "Gimme five," when nobody could hear you, "Time out," when nobody cared, "I need a second," when nobody gave a shit about how you felt, when they felt you break, "Help me," "Save me." The Girl on the Red Line Train, victim of the year, just another dumb bitch who couldn't stand up for herself: "Stop," "Time out," "Help me," maybe you deserved everything—

[ZORA *jumps to her feet, punching* MARK *in the stomach. FIGHT. Music rocks. Chairs are thrown, cartwheels are kicked, punches dodged, hits exploded. Finally,* ZORA *grabs a knife, kicks* MARK *to the ground, and kneels on his chest, the knife directly over his eye.*]

MARK AND ZORA: . . .

MARK: Lesson number thirty.

ZORA: I am not a victim,
    I am a fucking survivor,
    and that makes me unstoppable.

MARK: That was good. Zora, / that was good, that was good, I mean it,
    OK? That. Was. Good.

ZORA [*near tears*]: I am not a victim, I am a fucking survivor, / I fuck-
    ing survived, all that, all-of-that, I am not a victim, I am a fucking
    survivor, I am, I am, that's what I do, *goddamn it that's what I do.*

ANDY: That was awesome, like, really, really good, Zora, really really
    fucking awesome . . .

MARK: Time for a five.

ZORA: No breaks, no stops, no time for that: not anymore.

[ZORA *picks up a lead pipe.*]

    Both of you. Versus me.
    Two on one, same time, I'm right here.
    Come on. Come on. Come on. Come on. Come on.

[MARK *grabs a bat.* ANDY *picks up a broken chair.*]

ZORA: Oh my god. I love you guys so hard right now.

ANDY: Mutual feelings.

MARK: We got you.

EVERYONE: . . . AAAAAAAAAAAAAAH!

[*FIGHT! It's balls to the walls, no holds barred. Music blasts. Faces
get punched, bodies are thrown, this-hurts-a-lot. It doesn't stop until*

they're beat, exhausted, on the ground. Transition. For the first time they move in TOTALLY PERFECT formation!]

ALL: *Aaaaaaaaaaaaaaaaaaaaaaand—*
Punch, block, duck, weave
and punch, block, duck, weave
and punch, block, duck, weave.
Now cross it back and cross it over
up and down then start all over,
cross it back and cross it over, up and down, START ALL OVER.
Step it up then bring it down and flip and pose and touch the ground,
then pick it up and let it drop then flip it flip it flip it, STOP.
Just walk it off just walk it off just walk it off and
STOP
flex flex
take a break then check a text nah PSYCH
we bring it back we check on in we bring it back
and brace yourself, and brace yourself, and brace yourself, go on brace yourself then.
Punch, block, duck, weave
and punch, block, duck, weave
and punch, block, duck, weave.
Now cross it back and cross it over
up and down then start all over,
cross it back and cross it over, up and down, START ALL OVER.

[Transition. Beers. Blood. The sun sets behind them. They look messed up. Exhausted, they dance, they chant.]

ZORA, ANDY, MARK: *Get those bitches in the sack*
That's the way that we fight back!
Knock those fuckers outta whack.
That's the way that we fight back!

Sternum, heart, ass, dick, we won't stop we never quit, we'll bring
you down with just one hit, we're so supreme, the hottest shit.
So come at this watch us attack 'cause
That's the way that we fight back! (What!)
That's the way that we fight back! (Hey!)
That's the way tha—t

[*We hear gunshots, blocks away. Everybody stops.*]

ZORA: We need / to—

MARK: Don't move, stay up here, don't move, just hide, just / stay
here.

ANDY: "Just stay here."

ZORA: We-should-do-something, right now, / they can't be more than
three blocks away, MARK.

MARK: Get down, on the ground, ZORA, I SAID, GET DOWN . . .
Inside. Inside, right now.

[*More gunshots . . . Screaming . . . Sirens . . . MARK and ZORA exit, but*
ANDY takes one last look over the edge of the roof.]

ANDY: (Just leave us alone. *Leave us. Alone.*) JUST LEAVE US
ALONE. JUST LEAVE US ALONE, LEAVE US ALONE,
LEAVE-US-ALONE!

[*MARK carries out ANDY as he screams. He gives one final look back . . .*]

VOLUME 3

BACK ALLEY

[*That night.* JAX *sprays.* MARK *approaches.*]

JAX: Watch your step. Blood's not dry yet . . . Was wondering when you'd show up. Slurpee?

MARK: No thanks.

JAX: We don't continue this conversation without a Slurpee. We need props, otherwise we're just two brown men plotting something, it's all very simple and I got you: vanilla, to match your personality, bottoms up . . . Whiskey?

MARK: NO.
—Yes.

JAX: Quite literally it is the least I can do . . . So, is Farrington Park good enough for you? Half a block up, empty. If we're going to fight over what's good and what's bad, if we're gonna really do this then all I ask is that we relocate. This corner's seen enough blood tonight, so I'm recommending the park for fisticuffs.

MARK: I get it.
  Took me a while.
  Didn't want to.
  Now I get it.
  —So we don't forget.

JAX: Kind of my thing.

MARK: Nice work on your thing . . . Two people.

JAX: Three people were shot right where you're brooding.

MARK: Three people shot, but only two died.

JAX: So that's enough for you, right, you can sleep after "only two" because "least it's not three." . . . One was seventeen. Other one was twenty-three. Old lady was seventy-four, critical condition, Bellwether. Floor two, she'll be just fine, that's what you wanted, right, well now you have it, there you go, now, send on over some flowers and pat yourself on the back. She's gonna make it out just fine. You're welcome.

MARK: Three Lord Gang.

JAX: They do have a noticeable style don't they.

MARK: How many.

JAX: Six or seven.

MARK: That's it?

JAX: It never takes a lot of people to get together and do something stupid . . . two years ago the city came and they knocked down that school. "Big news," right? Nobody cared. Kids inside of it were supposed to transfer, some other place, six or seven miles, more west, they didn't, they got bored, they got bitter, and now they're grown and they're pissed but they are not stuck here, no, we are stuck here with them. Six or seven dumb fucks, by the end of the summer I'm sure it'll be three or four times that much.

MARK: How old.

JAX: Youngest is twenty.

MARK: What they drive?

JAX: They don't, they walk, the car used tonight was stolen.

MARK: Where they live at?

JAX: No.

MARK: I / said—

JAX: And I said no. I'm not telling you the location of your final rest-
ing place, / no—

MARK: We got this.

JAX: You mean the three of you—

MARK: We got this.

JAX: Nobody is afraid of Earth Wind and Afro, you are SCOOBIES, /
ohmygod, Ohmyfucking god—

MARK: Thank you for your help with the team name! / . . . Oh!
OK!—TOO SOON.

JAX: You want more, OK, what about DickLicking Pandas, Titty Trio,
or maybe you could just go by your birth name, and call yourself
The Weeknd. You can't just go over and take the rest of Up With
People, and try to solve their deep psychological issues with trust
falls and jazz hands, fuck no, homie, don't fold me like that, I am
not your map.

MARK: So when somebody else dies that's on your hands.

JAX: I instigate, I don't participate. / I—

MARK: You are complicit, you are responsible, *you watch.*

JAX: . . .

MARK: Day after tomorrow? Fourth of July, man. Used to be drunk motherfuckers and people out all night getting lit. This time, shit's gonna be real different, this time, they're gonna step it up, this time, they're gonna try and prove that they got what they got, *we can stop it* . . . 'Cause if we don't, then there will be bodies and blood and before you know it this place won't be ours, it will be theirs, and maybe that's what you want, 'cause you can finally say your signs were right, maybe that's just what you fucking want—

JAX: Thirty-two thirty-two Dalton Avenue South . . . Big house. Boarded-up windows. Empty for years, they found it, they moved in, they live and lie at thirty-two thirty-two Burnham Avenue South, follow the train, see—six stops down you can see it under the streetlight, right there, right there at thirty-two thirty-two Burnham Avenue South. No way to get in, there's a guy in the front, guy in the back, unless your faggotry can make you fly, you're fucked.

MARK: We don't need to fly, we just need to jump . . . Train stops right next to their house. Take that shit everyday, it goes close, platform not five feet away from their roof, and if the top floor has a window—Does their top floor got a window?

JAX: Their top floor has a big fucking window / (Ohmygoddddddddd.)

MARK: Then we jump into it and we do this. Late at night when they sleep, we beat the fuck out of them and on our way out we call the cops, 'cause if they wanna act like garbage men, then I say we put 'em to work. Temporary blows, no broken bones, nonlethal, mass impact, no guns, no bullets, enough of that, enough of that, we use what we got, we do the right thing.

JAX: And if a knockout punch turns into something a bit more lethal—

MARK: We stop before the blood goes black, I know how to do this—

JAX: 'Cause this isn't your first time, is it . . . Gotcha. See, at first, I thought you just watched too many Marvel movies and got high on the hype, but now I see it, now I know, no—their rage is not foreign to you, honey, their violence all too comfortable right here, honey—What they got, you still hold on to . . . What crew did you run with?

MARK: . . . Bloodline.

JAX: I remember Bloodline Gang, armed robbery, people screaming in the street, whatever happened to / them?

MARK: Had to.
Didn't want to, had to, where I'm from, had to. Ten years old, man, fucking ten years old.
Not like them. Nothing like them.
Said nothin' tho.
Complicit within it. *I started this* so I could help someone, so something bad never has to happen to anybody else.
"Literally, the least I can do."
—Thank you.

JAX: What color do you want me to tag their house after you die inside of it? I have red and black and green, that's it.

MARK: Hahahahahahaha.

JAX: If you want blue, then that's a special order and I'll have to take a trip to Jo-Ann Fabrics, what color do you want for your memorial?

MARK: Sorry, but I'm not going to give my last rites to someone who hides behind a mask, OK, it just seems very European, and I'd rather—

JAX [*taking off his mask*]: If they get the upper hand, they will kill you.
All of you.
And no one will ever know.

And I'll have to spray a sign on the side of their house,
for you, all of you, and that will make me very sad,
and when I get sad I get dark,
and when I get dark it's very very hard to pull me back into the
light,
or the shade,
or wherever I'm sitting right now, so just tell me what color, I need
to know the color, I have to know the color, 'cause if I don't know,
then I'll lose my patience, and when I lose my patience, I think
about my choices, and I've never been good at making choices, and
if I have to think about what I could or couldn't have done, then
I will go crazy again, this time for the last time, if you lose then I
will lose myself . . . Why can't you just move to Andersonville, just
buy a dog and feed a lesbian and move to fucking Andersonville.

MARK: Never seen you without the mask . . . You have, uh, you have—
I don't know, man, I don't—you have really nice eyes, / so . . .

JAX: That's gay.

MARK: Nuh-uh, / tho, nuh-uh.

JAX: Yeah huh, you're being real gay to me / right now.

MARK: I'm just / saying.

JAX: Stop looking at my eyes!

MARK: My bad, totally sorry.

JAX: Don't fuck this up, you stupid, stupid, stupid fuck.

MARK: Actually, I think you're supposed to say good luck?

JAX: Mark.

MARK: Jax.

JAX: *Please.*
    —Please don't die.

TRAIN PLATFORM

[*The next night, so late it's early.* ZORA *enters. She is slow but steady. A train passes, far, far away—she tightens up but doesn't wince.*]

ZORA: . . .

[ANDY *enters. Stands by her.*]

ZORA: It's always late, isn't it? Yeah.

ANDY: Yeah. Always, always late, yeah.

ZORA AND ANDY: . . .

ANDY: I bought candy. Just in case we, you know . . . just in case . . .
    You're not like a health nut are / you?

ZORA: No.

ANDY: Good, good. Good. Well. I have candy, so.

ZORA: Thank you.

ANDY: Oh, dollar five, there was a sale, / no biggie.

ZORA: Andy, shut up . . . The fuck is that bag.

ANDY: Oh! Oh, well, Mark told us to bring weapons, so I was googling, and the Google said that wasp spray is a powerful mix of chemicals and when it's shot into someone's eye, it can cause an attacker to have temporary blindness for up to ten minutes, so I got some jugs full of the stuff, hooked it up to these nozzle things, duck-taped it to this backpack, and on the outside it might make me look like a crazy person, but on the inside, I don't know man, I feel like really comfortable with my choices.

ZORA: . . . You do you, / honey.

ANDY: I am so doing the fuck out of me right now.

[*The train approaches. The soft sound of fireworks explodes in the distance.* MARK *enters. He stands with them. An unsteady calm: anxious, elated, cautious, apocalyptic.*]

EVERYONE: . . .

MARK: How long?

ZORA: . . . Twenty-two months. Six days. Since I've been on a goddamn train.

MARK: . . . That's long enough.

MARK AND ZORA: . . .

ANDY: . . . They changed the seats. It's like a, like a, like a subway now? Subway style now?

ZORA: OK.

ANDY: Yeah, I mean, it's all right.

ZORA: What about the smell?

ANDY: The—

ZORA: The smell, man, you know, the smell, / don't act stupid, you know the smell.

ANDY: Well, I mean, they clean it, usually, sometimes, it's not like / an ever present—

ZORA: That smell (you know that smell, goddamn it, Andy), it's thick and clean and rotten and sometimes when I'm in the shower, it comes right back in my nose, and my head gets dizzy and, can I sit down, / is there anywhere to sit, I, I, I . . .

MARK: You're fine standing, you're fine, you're fine. Zora. Zora, come on . . . OK, know what, nevermind, nevermind. Andy, take her arm, she needs to sit down. Zora, come on, you need to / sit down.

ZORA: Off me, OFF me . . . "I'm fine standing."

MARK: "Oh, k, all right, great, me too, I'm / good standing too."

ZORA: "All right, good then, you keep on standing then, that's good for you." Andy, how you doing?

ANDY: I'm having some candy and also standing.

MARK: He's fine.

ZORA: Damn right he's fine, he's standing.

MARK: Yeah he is.

ANDY: "Yay, ohmygod, we're so mighty."

[*The train approaches, loud and shaking. They step in.*]

TRAIN: "Doors Closing."

EVERYONE: . . .

ZORA: "Are we there yet?"

MARK: Two more stops.

ZORA: That's all?

MARK: . . . It's not too late. On the next one, if you guys . . . You want to. Guys. Come on. Not too late, and it's fine, and I'm good, on my own, I'm good, trust me, done this before, so you guys, on the next stop, just / go.

ANDY: I can't lose anybody else. Won't.

ZORA: . . . What he said.

MARK: . . . What he said.

MARK, ANDY, AND ZORA: . . .

ZORA: Did they suddenly just start letting people smoke on here? It's been / a while, but—

ANDY: Highly illegal, there's cameras now, did / you see when you—

MARK: Jesus Christ.

[JAX *enters from the back of the car, smoking . . . He takes off his mask.*]

JAX: . . . "I was in the neighborhood."

EVERYONE: . . .

MARK: If everyone listens to me and does exactly as I say,
    then I have no doubt in my mind that something up there, what-
    ever you want to call it—
    something bigger than us has our backs.
    Just listen to me. Follow my lead.
    This, all this? I've got this.

ZORA: What happens if you don't make it.

MARK: Not gonna happen.

ZORA: But if it happens then I'm just saying, so we know, if it happens then I take the lead, I get / us out—

MARK: Fuck no, Zora, you go too hard, you don't know how / to stop.

ZORA: I'm just saying tho, if they get you, Mark, if they *really get / you*—

MARK: If they get me then everyone here is *already dead.* My rules, my plan, we listen to me and only me, is that clear?

ZORA: I—

MARK: Is that clear.

ZORA: Right behind you. Whatever you do . . . But I'm just saying, / tho . . .

ANDY [*hands* JAX *a note*]: Ohmygod, ohmygod, please, please take this, OK, please, just—
My mom. Her address. Uh. So, if I die, please, give that to / my mom.

ZORA: Andy—

MARK: Just give it to me, Andy, I / got it.

ANDY: No, if I die, Jax, give that to my mom, the address is right on top. Mark, you *actually could die* and she could die *and I probably will die*, he can't die that's not what he does. *You'd leave us.* If things get rough in there, real rough in there, you'd run away, you'd just leave us all behind to die—

JAX: I—

ANDY: *But that's fine, OK*, that's fine because if it happens, then at least I'll know that you gave this to my mom, so she'd know what happened and she wouldn't worry about me anymore, she always worries about what's happening to me, but you can make sure that doesn't happen, so just, just, just *please*—give that to my mom.

JAX [*takes the note*]: . . . We don't die. We're Roustabouts. Not what we do.

MARK: . . . Roustabouts.
   —Roustabouts.

ZORA: Roustabouts.

ANDY: . . . *The* Roustabouts?

ZORA: / (Ohmygod, no, no.)

MARK: No "the," / Andy—

ANDY: Just Roustabouts, OK, OK, Roustabouts, singular? OK.

[*They suit up.* MARK *takes out his billy club, zips up his jacket.* ZORA *straps on two hand-held tasers and pulls down her hoodie.* ANDY *puts on his backpack, then straps a bottle behind his neck, full of fluid, with two cords connecting to wasp spray.* JAX *puts on his mask and pulls out his claws. They look terrifying and awesome.*]

TRAIN: "Doors Opening."

[*They rush out and jump off the platform.*]

VOLUME 4

TRAIN

[*Ten minutes later.* MARK, ZORA, ANDY, *and* JAX *board the train. Everybody looks like shit. Big black eyes, blood-stained T-shirts, ripped-apart pants, one or two missing shoes, limping, limping, limping. They sit in the exact same position as we last saw them.*]

EVERYONE: . . .

TRAIN: "Doors Closing."

EVERYONE: . . .

JAX: If this is what your God thinks "unscathed" looks like, I would like his address 'cause soon as I can walk, I'm gonna run over to his house and kick his ass.

EVERYONE [*a slow crack-up*]: . . . (*haahaahaha.*)
Hahahahaha.
HahahahaHAHAHAHAHAHAHAHAHAHAHAHAHAHAHAHA,
HAHAHAHHAHAHA / HAHA!

ANDY: Ow, ow, my back, / ow, my back, my baaaaaaaack.

ZORA: "My everything," / my fucking everything hurts, JESUS.

JAX: Suck it up, SUCK IT UP, all right, this is not the end of the world so just *DON'T touch me my shoulder is on fire, bitch,* / it hurts, OK, this ALL just HURTS.

ANDY: Is my cheekbone broken? Is that a thing? / Does it look broken?

MARK: "Is that a thing?"

JAX: I broke your cheekbone two weeks ago, the fat guy with the hammer put it back in place, / he did you a favor, *I broke it,* I'm the one, OK, just FYI—

ANDY: So it doesn't look weird or anything, everything's fine, / up here, everything—

MARK: Heyheyhey—

[They stare out the window; we see a quick flash of cop lights.]

EVERYONE: . . .

ZORA: Quickest I ever seen cops running. How'd you do that?

ANDY: I just *called them.*

ZORA: And?

ANDY: I said there was *trouble.*

ZORA: And?

ANDY: I told them that injustice was happening and they had to get there quick to / save the city.

ZORA: But for real tho.

ANDY: I said there was a big black gang and that a white person was in serious danger / and they FLEW DOWN THERE REAL QUICK.

EVERYONE: Hahahahahahahahahahahahahaha!

MARK: Can we smoke, can we smoke, please, / can we smoke, please, please, DAMN—

ANDY: Need a lighter? / ohmygod, jeez, takeittakeittakeit—

ZORA: Gimme that first. I need it first, / thank you, thank you very much.

MARK: Wow.

JAX: Can I say something?

ZORA: You can say anything.

JAX: OK, thank you, 'cause Goddamn Girl You Looked Fucked Up, / lemme just say, lemme just tell you how fucked up you look right now.

ANDY: *Hahahahahahaha / Hahahahahahahahaha!*

ZORA: I was being selfless, OK, they just came coming after me, / OK.

MARK: Maybe they wouldn't come after you if you didn't start screaming, "I'M THE ONE YOU WANT / I'M RIGHT HERE, I'M RIGHT HERE!"

JAX: Hahaa / hahahahaha you did, tho, you did that shit!

ZORA: FUCK YOU, I did a good job, right, / I did OK in there, right?

MARK: You kicked ass.

JAX: Ass was kicked, / ass was most definitely kicked.

ZORA: Everybody did, / everybody here kicked ass.

MARK: Ass was kicked!

JAX: Ass was kicked!

EVERYONE: *Ass was KICKED! Wooooooooooo!*

ANDY: *Hahahahahahahahahaha,* ha ha . . . ha . . . I, I actually need to go to the hospital. So, at this next / stop—

MARK: No hospitals. No paper trail. Go home, fix yourself up, we got out of there fine.

ZORA: And Nina's gonna need you back at nine to nine-thirty so you'd better come at nine to nine-thirty 'cause people need to stick to schedules.

ANDY: . . . *Hahahahahahaha / hahaha.*

ZORA: I'm not kidding.

ANDY: Fuck my life.

TRAIN: "Doors Opening."

ANDY: . . . Anybody else feel like they could just take over the whole goddamn world, but also so sick you could just throw up every-where? I can't be the only one. Like, it can't be just me.

[JAX *takes out a bottle of Vicodin. Pours a handful out to* ANDY.]

TRAIN: "Doors Closing."

[ANDY *exits.*]

MARK AND ZORA: . . .

ZORA: What's next.

MARK: Shower. Sleep. Wake up. Work.

ZORA: Then what?

MARK: Sleep, wake up, shower, work.

ZORA: Then?

MARK: "Then, I dunno, maybe go see a movie in the park," / who knows—

ZORA: Mark. What's next.

MARK: You're fired up.

ZORA: I'm fired up.

MARK: All woke now / and shit.

ZORA: Been woke and stayed like that, mafucker, I / am on fire right now, boy, I am on FLAME—

MARK: Feeling that rush, that high feeling your heart, like it won't stop.

JAX: She's got a taste in her mouth.

ZORA: Damn right.

JAX: I'd say spit, 'cause you have no fucking clue what you're 'bout to swallow.

ZORA AND JAX: . . .

ZORA: HAHAHAHAHA / HAHAHAHAHAHAHAHAHAHAHA HAHAHAHAA.

JAX: HAHA / HAHAHAHAHAHAHAHHAHAHAHAHAHAHA HAHA.

MARK: Hahaaha this actually seems pretty tense, so I don't know why we're laughing, but all right!

ZORA: Tomorrow night, eight o'clock, the roof. Our bodies need it. Our heads need it. My mind fucking needs this, Mark, my mind fucking needs *this*.

MARK: . . . The roof.

ZORA: The roof.

MARK AND ZORA: "Let's take it to the roof, let's take it to the roof." / Yeeeeeeeeeah. "The roof, the roof."

TRAIN: "Doors Opening."

ZORA: . . . You look better with the mask on.

JAX: You looked better in 1998 on season three of *Moesha*, mmmk, bye, Felicia.

ZORA: . . . You're good, / damn.

JAX: I know right.

ZORA: He's good, you're good, we good, Roustabouts mafucker!

MARK: Sssssssh / shut the fuck up girl! (Shut the fuck up!)

ZORA: Sorry (sorry sorry sorry), I AM THE GIRL FROM THE RED LINE TRAIN! "I don't want nobody fucking with meeeeee in these streets!"

[*She's gone.*]

JAX: Can I be real with you? . . . Baking soda. For your face. Just put a bunch in the sink and dunk your head in. It burns, obviously.

MARK: Did I do good?

JAX: I don't pat backs, I bash skulls.

MARK: Knock it.

JAX: Knock / what?

MARK: The sass and the low blows, you wanna be real with me?

JAX: I'm trying.

MARK: Then look me in the eye, listen to my shit, you wanna be real with me, then be real with me.

. . . That *rage*? That. That thing, in me, that—
That, that, that fire, that heat, that bomb going off—
Felt it everyday when I rolled, when I fought, when I . . .
I lost it. Did my work and became somebody else and I lost it and
I never looked for it again, never needed it again, but back there
man, back there—
I felt it again and I saw it in Zora and I saw it in Andy and for
them it's new and if they don't get how to separate that, then
they won't know what to do with it when it comes up again, and
if it comes up again / then—

JAX: It won't.

MARK: They can't control it, they don't know how to use it.

JAX: That's why they have you.

MARK: They need better than me they / need—

JAX: They do, they need the best and you're not the best, you've
fucked up before, you're a mess, but know what, *You're what we
got*, and tonight you did good, Mark. Tonight you did real, real,
real good.

MARK: . . . You did good, / too, Jax.

JAX: Fucking mutual admiration society / over here.

MARK: No, you did, you showed up when you didn't have to and you
helped and you did something good—

JAX: There was a second when everyone was down on the ground, and
you guys didn't look like you were gonna make it, there was a
split second where I wanted to run.

MARK: But *you didn't*. OK, you didn't. We're the same now.

JAX: You have a conscience, I do not.

MARK: Bullshit, you pulled two guys off of me, we fought side by side, Zora tripped, you helped her back up, come on, man, you give several fucks, *you care*—

JAX: *I can't.* No room for it, *I can't* . . . People seem nice, at first, real nice, good, even. Then you get to know them and they turn on you or they move away from you or they die on you and then all that time with them, all that trust, all the care wasted, gone, shit to show for it, *too expensive,* I've done it before and it wiped me out, it is expensive to give a shit and I'm broke.

MARK [*reaching for his forehead*]: There's blood on / your—

JAX: *I can get it,* I can get it, don't.

[JAX *wipes his forehead.*]

MARK AND JAX: . . .

MARK: So you done with us now? This is it then?

JAX: This is it.

MARK: Well, all right then.

JAX: That's right . . . Unless you wanna do some real shit.

MARK: We gotta go back to basics, back to training, gonna take some time.

JAX: Nevermind then—

MARK: But I'm open for suggestions.

JAX: . . . I say we skip this hood, skip the little shit, I say we go all the way to the top.

MARK: Oh you got plans / —hahahahahahhaa!

JAX: Oh I have definite plans for Charlie's Faggots, let's go full on *Fight Club* and start at the top:
DONALD—
"Donald Trump."

JAX: Donald fucking Trump—

MARK: Fuck that mother / fucker—

JAX: Fuck that motherfucker, know what I say?

MARK: What you / say?

JAX: I say we scale the side of that tower downtown, spray-paint the fuck out of it, and turn that big "T" into a sideways vagina.

MARK: I'm in.

JAX: Damn right you're in, see, we go big, we go hard, let's go now, OK, I've got grappling hooks and—

[MARK *grabs* JAX *and kisses him.* JAX *pulls back. Slaps him.*]

JAX: I'm sorry, but, Who the hell do you think I am? Use your fucking tongue.

[JAX *jumps on* MARK; *they make out hardcore.*]

TRAIN: "Doors Closing."

ROOFTOP

ANDY: ACUTALLY AWESOME TRAINING MONTAGE! PART TWO!

[*Montage spans several weeks. Music. One by one, they enter in their Final Costumes. It's tight.*]

EVERYONE: *That's the way, that that's the way, that that's the way that we fight back.*

JAX: Transition!

[*Transition.*]

MARK: When I blow the whistle you have fifteen seconds, at the end of fifteen seconds we will have a winner. No holds, no stops, no time out's, no re-do's, five, four, three, two, one! / [*Blows whistle*] Fifteen, fourteen, thirteen, twelve, eleven, ten, nine, eight, seven, six, five, four, three, two, one—

ZORA, ANDY, JAX: AAAAAAAAAAAA!

[MARK *blows the whistle, and* ZORA, ANDY, *and* JAX *attack each other. Everyone is down on the ground but* ANDY.]

ANDY: Ohmygod, did I win, did I actually win?

[ZORA *kicks him, he falls over like a sack of potatoes. She rises.*]

ZORA: Yes! SECOND PLACE!

ANDY: That's not a thing!

MARK: New Rule: second place is NOW A THING.

ZORA: BOO-YA, / told you so, told you so, BITCH. OHHHHHH, treated! "Second place, in your face. Second place, go SECOND PLACE!"

JAX: Jesus Christ / in a cast iron crutch SHUT UP (this is terrible) SHUT UP; also, NO DANCING.

ANDY: THAT'S GREAT / BUT I'M STILL FIRST PLACE SO WHATEVER ABOUT EVERYTHING!

MARK: Everybody back to your positions, we do this again in five, four, three, two, one!

[*Transition.*]

[MARK *throws a duffel bag of props in front of the team.*]

MARK: Today's lesson: Lying to the Police. Grab a prop, don't stop what you're doing, Andy on questions, get an alibi in five, four, three, two, one!

ANDY: "Ms. Zora, for the sake of the record, please tell me where you were during the events of February fourteenth of this year."

ZORA: "It was Valentine's Day, right? Not like I remember, I spend all day at home with my cats and cheese because I'M THE GIRL FROM THE RED LINE TRAIN, LEAVE ME ALONE."

MARK: Case dismissed, NEXT!

ANDY: "Jax, have you ever—"

JAX: No.

ANDY: "We have a record of—"

JAX: No.

ANDY: "There is photographic evidence—"

JAX: Where?

ANDY: Right here.

JAX: That's not me.

ANDY: It's not?

JAX: RACIST!

MARK: Case dismissed, NEXT!

[*Transition.*]

JAX: OK class, today I'm taking over for Mark because apparently we need to take this shit to the next level and to do that you need a big shovel, enter me.

ANDY: Ohmygod best name ever, you're the Shoveler!

ZORA: No code names.

ANDY: Yeah says *the Girl from the* / *Red Line Train.*

ZORA: ANDY THE BED WETTING BITCH.

JAX: SHUT UP, look, a couple weeks ago you broke into a house with a bunch of sleeping gang members and beat them up, congratulations, you got lucky. Today's lesson is in stamina, today's lesson is about winning. No weapons, no special effects, just you, you, and you. It's everybody for themselves, ready?

ZORA: Ready!

ANDY: Ready!

MARK: Ready.

JAX: (You're slouching again.)

MARK: (Am I, *shit*, sorry.)

JAX: (It's OK, breathe / from here, there you go.)

MARK: (Breathe from here, I got it.)

JAX: (You got it?)

MARK: Ready!

JAX: A five, six, seven, eight!

[MARK, ZORA, *and* ANDY *fight. With little to no competition,* MARK *knocks them to the ground and stands triumphant.*]

Ladies and gentlemen, we have a winner: Mark, take a bow; Zora, don't duck when you can kick; Andy, learn how to use your body in a way that does not bring to mind a soft pretzel from the state fair.

ANDY: I'M GOING THROUGH POST TRAUMATIC STRESS.

ZORA: TAKE SOME PILLS.

ANDY: OK, THANK YOU, THAT SOLVES EVERYTHING.

JAX: A five, six, seven, eight!

[*Transition.*]

[MARK *and* JAX *drinking.* MARK *throws down a set of keys.*]

JAX: Not cute. What are these for?

MARK: Typically they are used to both open and lock / doors.

JAX: Why'd you give them to me. / Why. Why. Why.

MARK: Fuck, uh, I don't know, thought you could run me a bath, open a beer, record / some TV—

JAX: This a trap?

MARK: What?

JAX: I go into your place and there's like a booby trap or a collapsible floor, / that it?

MARK: Oh, Jax, totally.

JAX: You call the cops, some people I pissed off, some store I tagged, "Here's the address, he's got keys, go get him."

MARK: Can you slow / the fuck down—

JAX: This is a threat, OK, you have just handed me a threat, so I have to proceed with caution or else I'm dead, not my time, not yet, now, what the hell are these for because I am very confused right now and when I get confused I get, I get . . .

MARK: . . . Sometimes you don't pick up. And I hear a siren. Hear a gunshot. Sometimes we go to bed, and when I wake up, you're gone, and it's raining. Sometimes, I want to come home and see that you're already there. —Not every time. Not all in. I don't know. Just sometimes. But hey, if you don't—

[JAX *kisses* MARK . . . *drops the keys back in his hand.*]

JAX: Whenever you want me, just leave the window open. I don't do doors.

ALDERMAN'S OFFICE

[*The next night.* ZORA *is setting up a manila folder full of, like, professional-looking business shit.* ANDY *looks like hell on earth.* JAX *drinks in the corner.*]

ANDY: . . . I told Nina I was a superhero.
   That's crazy, right?
   I told my boss that I spent my nights on a roof running around training, fighting, busting up perps, and saving the city.
   I told my boss that I've had two concussions, twenty-three stitches, a broken knee, and a mild seizure, none of which has been professionally treated.
   I told our boss that you were by my side the whole time, and together we were doing twice as much as any alderman, told her we were, were unstoppable, I told Nina fucking Esposito that we're so tight that we make Judge Dredd look like Club Med—
   I told my boss we were superheroes.

ZORA: . . . And what'd she say?

ANDY: She said I must be smoking some good shit and asked me to give her some for free.

ZORA: Fuck that old lady.

ANDY: OHHHHHH! / Yes yes yes!

ZORA: Fuck her, fuck her to hell, fuck all her shit, enough of it, I'm DONE: Warpath mafucker!

ANDY: Warpath!

ZORA: (OK too much tho.)

ANDY: (Warpath.)

ZORA: There you go, so: I got some plans.

ANDY: Yeah you do!

ZORA: Been thinking about this since The Night We Won. Big plan, good plan, workable plan but I need you to wingman me on this all right.

ANDY: Fuck yeah, we going to Big Shitty Tap, they love me / there.

ZORA: No we're not going to bitty shitty tap, also you need to stop going to Big Shitty Tap—

ANDY: When I walk in, they greet me like I'm Norm from *Cheers*.

ZORA: FOCUS, Andy. Goddamn, you got crazy eyes lately and I don't need any crazy eyes right now, I need focused shit from you, that's it 'cause if you start—sorry. Know what, I'm / sorry for that.

ANDY: No, it's OK.

ZORA: No, I shouldn't have said that, OK, that's bull, I'm just like, I'm just like charged as fuck right lately, OK, and I gotta keep that for myself, I can't put that on you, you do you 'cause you're good and you're feeling it and you're doing just fine—

ANDY: No I'm not.
. . . But that, that's OK, though, that's just how I'm—that's fine. And I will focus.

Not a—that is not an easy thing to, uh, hard for me, lately,
difficult, OK, but worth it, right, it's—
I can focus. I can do that.
Worth it, right?

ZORA: Totally, totally worth / it.

[MARK *enters.*]

MARK: All right, let's get this off the ground. Just 'cause it's raining
out, don't mean we can't bring it (amiright?). SHADAT, Backhand, ramping. Up up up, everybody, up up up, let's go—

ZORA: I have a proposition . . . Just: just hear me out.

JAX: . . . Is this turning into a meeting?

ZORA: This is turning into a / meeting.

JAX: OK, I don't do meetings, have so much fun—

MARK: Hold up.

JAX: Oh no, I can't, "meetings," no no no, and I would, if I could,
believe me I would love nothing more than to sit around a circle
and kumbaya right now with *Bébé's Kids,* but last time I had to sit
through a meeting I picked up the table, threw it across the room,
and punched everybody in the face, everybody, just right down
the row, bambambam, so many cubicles, you know, so no, no, I
can't, really, no.

MARK: . . . When the hell did you have a sit-down job?

ZORA: Who even asked you to be here?

ANDY: Yeah and what the fuck is *Bébé's Kids*?

MARK / ZORA / JAX [*variously*]: WHOOOA / Oh hell nah, HELL
fucking nah. / READ A BOOK, read a fucking BOOK.

MARK: Look, OK, first things first. Number one, Zora, I call breaks, I
call propositions, I call all this shit. Number two, Jax, you don't
leave until I dismiss you, that's final, and number three, Andy,
I can suddenly tell everything about you 'cause if you never
watched *Bébé's Kids* then you never had a soul, / OK, all right,
that's what's up right now.

ZORA: / Tell him! Tell him!

JAX: I'm so disappointed in you.

MARK: Zora—two minutes.

ZORA: Andy. Time me.

ANDY: On it, / totally, totally on it.

JAX: (Such pageantry happening over here, / oh my god.)

ANDY [*on his phone*]: Two minutes aaaand—go.

ZORA: 'Bout a month ago we did something awesome, all right.
We suited up, we jumped on a train, we beat the enemy till they
couldn't walk and now those bitches are locked the fuck up, we
won.
Crime is down, fuckery is down, I haven't heard a bullet on any
of our blocks IN WEEKS, we-did-something-good.
—But now we're back to step one.
Back to push-ups and backhand and running around blocks,
nothing wrong with that, that's foundation, that's important.
—But so is protecting what we can,
when we can,
with what we have, and for once, for once, we have it.
So:
I wanna make a list.
A list of all the corrupt, useless, back-stabbing mafuckers within a
two-mile radius,

from the top of the top, to the bottom dwelling what not's, I
wanna make a list 'cause
this is our one shot to fix something we've been told is unfixable.
Nothing is unfixable, not anymore.
So I say we put our heads together,
I say we make this shit legit,
I say we take what we have and we do whatever we can do to do
something—
before it gets too late to do shit but shit.
. . . How we on time?

ANDY: Fifty-eight seconds to spare.

ZORA: All right, then you have one minute to hit me.
—Verbally, not literally, please, / OK, was that clear?

ANDY: (Maybe try "comments, views, opinions")

ZORA: (That's good, OK, thank you.) Anyone got comments, views,
opinions?

ANDY: "CVO?"

EVERYONE: . . .

JAX: . . . Meetings have gotten so weird now.

ZORA: How many walls you spray this week? Eight? Nine?

JAX: I memorialized six different / locations with—

ZORA: That's six people dead, in this neighborhood, that you know of,
Tuesday, enough. Enough small impact, enough waiting for someone to do something, so that we may react, we got it, let's use it,
we pick the mark, we choose it, enough sitting around in a circle
chanting some bullshit about what we're all about, if we about
this then let's be about / this—

MARK: *Enough.* How we doing on time here, Andy?

ANDY: Uh, we're past / time.

MARK: I gave you two minutes, you had two minutes, now you give me the floor. Enough. We had one shot. We took it. It worked.

ZORA: Well aware—

MARK: Now you're coming to me, trying to take this up to two, when I don't think you realize how lucky we got with the one / I—

ZORA: So this is about fear with you—

MARK: Whoa, I'm Sorry, / what?

ZORA: I mean, either you have a problem with my idea, or you've already thought of this idea before and you're just afraid to use it, so, / I think it must be about fear with you.

MARK: What part of "enough" don't you understand, / I SAID ENOUGH.

ANDY: Dude, come on, let her / finish—

MARK: Stay in your lane, / Andy, this zero—

ANDY: No, for real, let her finish, I mean, like, *what the fuck is your problem*, man, for real, for fucking real, and don't 'Andy' me, OK, just don't, don't do it, I know I'm dumb and I can't keep up and I'm white and I'm weird and I don't know what the hell a Bebe's Kid is but don't talk to me like I'm not part of this, I'm part of this, OK, I've been part of this from the start of this and when you talk to me like that, when you, when you just treat me like that, like I don't have something to say, like I don't, like I don't . . .

MARK [*calm*]: Andy, put your weapon down.

[ANDY *has grabbed onto his spray during the monologue. He doesn't realize it until it's pointed out . . . He drops it.*]

ANDY: I didn't mean . . . I didn't mean to like . . .

MARK: Go home. Pack up, get out, go the fuck home.

ANDY: . . . I'm sorry. I'm just, I'm just, I'm—

[ANDY *exits.*]

MARK: . . . Go with him, that boy is fucked up lately, for real, go.

JAX: . . .

MARK: "Please."

JAX: There you go, see. That gets you everything.

ZORA: . . . Mmmhmmm.

MARK: "Mmmhmmm," fuck you doing tonight, girl?

ZORA: Oh come on now don't act brand new, / Mark.

MARK: I'm trying to keep up but when you jump from zero to sixty
    on me, I gotta pull back and ask some serious, serious fucking /
    questions.

ZORA: Everyone's got a list. You know this. Anyone, with any power,
    from the mayor to the governor; my boss, alderman of dumbfuck,
    has a list, and I see it, but nobody-wants-to-act.

MARK: Why.

ZORA: They're scared.

MARK: Not you, though.

ZORA: Hell nah, see, I run shit now. The fuck do I have left to be
    scared of?

MARK: Come at me.

ZORA: . . .

MARK: Go ahead, come at me. You got your weapons on you, right? Told you not to bring 'em around anymore but I see, I know, *let's go*, whip 'em out, put 'em up, I'm good with just my hands, don't worry—come at me.

ZORA: . . . I get it.

MARK: Then let's go.

ZORA: Trying to put me in my place, trying to show me what's up, / I get it.

MARK: That's not what's up.

ZORA: You want to knock me down so I get back in line, that's what's happening, I / get it.

MARK: Kick My Ass. You run shit now, you hold it down now, you wanna take control now, wanna lead the team, you wanna rock your list, all right then, make me fall in line. You want something left to be scared of, well, all right then. Come at me.

MARK AND ZORA: . . .

ZORA: Your fly's undone.

MARK: No it's not—

ZORA: Yeah it is.

MARK: Nuh-uh.

ZORA: Yeah huh.

MARK: Nuh-uh.

ZORA: Nigga please, nigga please.

[MARK *zips his fly.*]

MARK AND ZORA: . . .

ZORA: So, we good here?

MARK: "So we good here."

ZORA: You're *family* . . . That's respect. That's that deep, deep shit. That's love.

MARK: Same.

ZORA: Good, but Mark, please know that was the first and last time you ask me to fight you, because the next time you do, I will accept that challenge and it will not end well for you.

MARK AND ZORA: . . .

MARK: Whiskey? . . . Whiskey? You want whiskey?

ZORA: Oh I got whiskey / all right . . .

MARK: Damn! Where you hide that?

ZORA: I built a side holster thing, you've / seen my side holster thing—

MARK: I thought that was for weapons.

ZORA: Whiskey is a weapon, / OK, whiskey is very much a weapon.

MARK: Put yours up.

ZORA: "Put yours up."

MARK: Raise it up, raise it up. / "Raise it UP!"

ZORA: To what, bitch, to what?

MARK: The end. Next week, last class, last session, last montage thing, whatever the fuck—we said for the summer. Next week's Labor Day, so: the end.

ZORA: . . . Work tomorrow. Early, early, / early—

MARK: Oh come / ON, Zora!

ZORA: Don't try it, / Mark, don't—

MARK: Come on, / the least you can do—

ZORA: Gotta get up, gotta head up, can't just drink myself to sleep every day of the week. Besides, that smells like bottom shelf, miss me on that, / so—

MARK: That's how it is.

ZORA: "That's how it is." ... Friday Night.

MARK: Don't do anything stupid before then please.

ZORA: ... "Friday Night."

STOOP

[*Meanwhile,* JAX *and* ANDY *chill the fuck out. We hear a car pass, LOUD music.*]

ANDY: Hey! It's eleven at night, OK, KEEP IT THE FUCK DOWN!

[*Car passes.*]

JAX: . . . I like that song.

ANDY: Oh, I do too, I've got like four remixes of it, it's great, but, you know, it's eleven and it's Tuesday so there's like an established status quo. Don't worry about it, they heard me, totally taken care of.

JAX: Mmmhmm?

ANDY: Yeah yeah yeah, I got it, totally. All good man don't you even worry, I got it, and if—

[*Car passes, slow.* ANDY *stands . . . Car drives off.*]

—See? We're all good.

JAX [*big inhale*]: So, Andy: this is an intervention.

ANDY: Sweet.

JAX: Yeah, this is a—this is kind of a big "come to Jesus" thing here, kid, real "batten down the hatches" / stuff here, all right?

ANDY: Totally, totally, I am all about the hatches.

JAX: Right?

[JAX *takes out a flask.*]

I worry about your safety.

ANDY: *Aw!*

JAX: And I don't worry about a lot of stuff, / either, OK.

ANDY: You don't, you really / don't.

JAX: Don't care! I should! But I Don't! Can't. Not enough room for it. But your safety? Your well-being?

ANDY: "My fierce moves, my rockin bod, this fine white ass."

JAX: Your sanity.

ANDY: I'm totally sane.

JAX: Self diagnosed.

ANDY: Yeah and my doctor is awesome, so don't worry about / it.

JAX: I just—

ANDY: Don't Worry About It . . . Jeez. And I'm sorry. But Jax? You? Of all people—

JAX: Am maybe the only one in the correct position to see what's happening—

ANDY [*sharp*]: Well, the first time I met you, uh, you acted like a deranged lunatic and you looked evil and you kicked the shit out of me, but now, oh, now you troll my Facebook and like, like, like everything, like we're like friends or something and—

JAX: . . .

ANDY: And I mean *we are*. OK, we are, but—I didn't mean it / like that—

JAX: Andy: what have you been up to after the sun sets?

ANDY: . . .

JAX: Word on the street is that there's some dumb kid running around Rightlynd late-late night, wearing a silly little jacket, patroling like the police,
this dumb kid has a costume.
This dumb kid is the only white person on a brown brown block:
This *stupid*, stupid, dumb little boy, with a death wish, without *a brain*, this fucking IDIOT…
has a theme song.

[ANDY *presses a button on his jacket. He's got a speaker hooked into his hoodie. We hear Kendrick Lamar's "King Kunta."*]

ANDY: . . . You gotta, you gotta wait for the verses / to actually—

JAX: My dick has already gone inside my body to hide, / *too late for the verses.*

ANDY: Look, I am activated and I have to do something about that / or else.

JAX: I'm sorry, didn't you just beat the fuck out of some gang members last month / or was that some other motherfucker?

ANDY: Last month, OK, last month—not every night, right now everything's getting back to normal, OK, we did one thing, and it helped a little, for a second, but that can't hold, OK, people are still out there, and before they do something to somebody else I—I'm just doing whatever I can so that doesn't happen.

JAX: I am / too.

ANDY: Not like me.

JAX: Christ, this subplot is boring as fuck, ohmygod, when is this out of your system? This whole darkest timeline thing, with the un-sexy drinking, the back talking, the fistfuls after fistfuls of drugs that should only go one / by one.

ANDY: Well they're the only thing helping me right now / so—

JAX: I'm helping / you.

ANDY: You can't help anybody, that's not what you do, you don't know how, I—
I,
I'm scared.
I'm really, really scared man, I'm—
I see stuff.
OK?
I said OK, / OK?

JAX: OK.

ANDY: OK?
Not like crazy stuff, not like I'm hallucinating, I see—
. . . When we did that thing.
On the train.
"When we won."
I remember one of those—I remember one of those guys, when we first went into the window, and we spread out, and we just started punching and kicking, I remember this guy.

This kid.

Maybe nineteen, maybe twenty.

This kid

was sleeping on like the couch, just sleeping, and we ran in and he got up,

covered in tattoos,

he got up and he reached for something, he reached for his,

reached for his backpack, his bag, "reached for a gun," I thought,

he's reaching for a gun.

So I run up to him and I have my spray and I'm running and running and it's too late 'cause he's already in his backpack and I spray from five feet away.

Knocks him right in the face and he screams and I throw the cans down and jump on top of him and punch and punch and punch and I hear Mark,

"Get up get out,"

And I get up but right before I get out I turn around and I look and this kid's hand's out of his backpack and—

And he was holding glasses.

We ran in, and woke him up, and he reached for his glasses and he couldn't see.

This kid

Didn't know what hit him.

Why.

How it happened, what time it was, where he was, he, he, he, he—

He just needed his glasses.

. . . Think he's got an eye patch now.

JAX: Hahaha what? What, like a fucking pirate or some shit?

ANDY: No just tape right over his eye 'cause it's always bleeding, 'cause it / still hurts—

JAX: Hahaha, who the hell told you that shit?

ANDY: I saw him two nights ago, it's clearly visible.

JAX: . . .

ANDY: The cops got five people when we won that night, right, uh, they booked 'em, and they're behind bars, they're locked up for a while, I know.

. . . But there were *six people* in that house.

. . . I had on the handkerchief. But right before I sprayed him it dropped and he, he saw me and—

And now *we see each other*. On the street.

And he doesn't do anything, he just looks, and sometimes he comes by in a car, and he just looks, he stares at me.

And he doesn't know that I watched my two friends die last year and then tried to help other people so they wouldn't have to hurt anymore, all he knows is that he watched his friends get beat the fuck up and then arrested and then put away. All he knows is that he hurts, like I did, just like I did, but his is worse because he doesn't know where to put it. *So I gotta be tough,* and I gotta keep training, and I gotta keep walking the street so I can save other people so I can make up for what I did because I can't shake it. *I see him,* I see him everywhere.

I can see him I can see him I can see him and I, I, I, I don't know what to do anymore, / I, I, I, I, I—

JAX: (I know you don't, / I know, I know.)

ANDY: *I don't know what to do, I don't, I don't, / I don't, I don't, I don't know what to do.*

JAX: I know, kid, I know. I know.

[ANDY *falls onto* JAX's *shoulder, emotional collapse.* JAX *doesn't move.*]

Shhhhh. It's OK. It's OK. It's OK.

. . . OK? You're good, / OK? You're good.

ANDY: I'm OK, I'm good, / sorry, I'm—

.

JAX: You're good, look at you, sit up, smoke this, you're totally good.

[ANDY *composes himself. They smoke.*]

Know what you're gonna do?

ANDY: Ohmygod, please tell me.

JAX: You're gonna go inside.

ANDY: I'm gonna go inside.

JAX: You're gonna pack up / your stuff—

ANDY: I'm gonna pack up / my stuff—

JAX: You're gonna give back those Vicodin pills you stole from me last
    week—

ANDY: That was an / accident though.

JAX: You're gonna take your stolen Vicodin and you're going to chop
    them up and put them in ice cream and put that ice cream in a to
    go cup and you're going to be the only person who has ever seen
    where I live.
    Because it's not safe here, not anymore, you're going to go to my
    couch and you're going to sleep.
    Then tomorrow you're gonna wake up.
    And you're going to get on the train.
    And you're gonna go back to fucking Schaumburg and your mom
    is going to call the police and they're gonna find that guy with
    the one eye and then you can come back here and rejoin your
    friends on the roof for the last time you all do the Mighty Mor-
    phin Fosse Fosse.
    . . . That's your next twenty-four hours.
    We leave in two minutes.

ANDY: For real?

JAX: For real for real, I cannot tell a lie, it's Tuesday.

ANDY: Ha.

JAX: And don't tell Mark. I'll tell Mark. He likes getting information in a sassy yet confident and expressive manner.

ANDY: Oh yeah?

JAX: That's how all the Wayans brothers are, oh yeah.

ANDY: Teeheheheehehehheehehehe, oh my god do you love him?

[JAX *slaps* ANDY, *hard, across the face.*]

JAX [*middle school girl*]: . . . Like, duh.

ANDY: Called it! Called it!
   . . . You should tell him.

[*We hear a car slow riding, closer, closer.*]

JAX: You should shut up and pack a bag, / we leave in two minutes—

ANDY: No, you should tell him, and then you should get matching outfits and turn into like a tag team.

JAX: Trust me when I say that we are already a tag team.

ANDY: Eww! Awesome!

JAX: You think Zora knows?

ANDY: Well, she's got eyes and a nose, I mean you two are really bad at covering up your sex—

JAX: *I have one suit*, OK, / I would have to wash it like daily.

ANDY: I've got four outfits that look exactly like this, it saves so much time. Zora says once she gets the grant then we can just have like a row of suits, like a whole fucking row—

JAX: Jesus damn. If she wants to be Professor X so bad I will PUT her into a wheelchair, / I mean, my god.

ANDY: It's next-level stuff here, so don't tell her I told you, but for real like a / whole entire—

JAX: It's not actually a costume if you have an entire—

ANDY: GET DOWN!

[ANDY *throws* JAX *to the ground at the last second. GUNSHOT. GUN-SHOT. GUNSHOT.*]

VOLUME 5

STOOP

[*A week later.* ZORA *enters.* MARK *enters.* JAX *enters. He crosses to the stoop . . . He sprays an A.*]

EVERYONE: . . .

ZORA: There we go.

EVERYONE: . . .

ZORA: There we go.

EVERYONE: . . .

ZORA: Last session, right? Labor Day. You said till the end of summer and it's Labor Day, so.

MARK: . . .

ZORA: Please.
Right after this we—
We go to the roof, we lay it down, just like we used to, and we get some kinda—
Some kinda—

I need it. I really, really: one last time.
For Andy, all right, Andy woulda wanted it like / that—

JAX: *You keep his name out your mouth.*
This will be the last moment we spend together so please, just please . . .
Do not pretend like you know shit you most certainly do not, you, it is over, it is done, can't you fucking see that this shit stops now . . .
You keep his name
out your / mouth.

MARK: *Hey.*
. . . I know, k. I know. I know that right now, that everything—

[ZORA *swiftly exits.*]

. . . You did a—you did a good thing here, OK, it—it looks good, Jax. You did a good thing here, and I want / you to—

JAX: *BACK the fuck up, backthefuckup.*

MARK AND JAX: . . .

JAX: I went
to Schaumburg.
I took the train and I did the walk and I went
to a house
in Schaumburg
to tell a woman that her son,
her stupid, stupid, stupid son,
had died.
And I knocked on the door and she opens it and I'm just about to tell her how her son stepped over the line, how he fucked up, how he failed so fast how, how he was dumb and average, just average in every way, just unremarkable and high and lost *and he was my favorite,* he was my my my he was my—

I start *crying*.

And she starts *crying*.

And I gave her the note, and we just sat down, together, on the steps, not touching not looking, just crying.

. . . I didn't say a word.

I just got up to go,

and she said "thank you" and she grabbed me and she hugged me and she held me for . . .

I left.

And on my way back to the train, I see all these people looking out their windows.

And by the time I get down the block there's a cop car.

"Neighbors said they saw you grabbing some lady, who are you, where are you going."

No mask. No weapons. I ran, so fast, through backyards and alleys and I ran and ran until I got to a place where I could blend in with just my skin.

I got the fuck out of Schaumburg.

. . . You did this.

You made me try to do something better.

It got me broken bones and dodging bullets and human contact and whiskey and Schaumburg and blood on my hands, blood on my conscience, which I now have, in me, and it sucks and it's scary there, there's blood in there, and blood back in my heart. *I hurt*, so, much, and I will never, ever forgive you for any of what you gave to me *do not look for me* do not send for me, if you do I will find you first, and I will bring you all the pain you gave to me, *just give me up, JUST GO.*

MARK: . . . I left the window open.

Every night.

JAX: Summer's over . . . Shut it up.

[MARK *exits.* JAX *stares at the stoop . . . Puts on the mask. Disappears.*]

ROOFTOP

[*That night.* ZORA, *already on the roof.* MARK *enters. They're feeling the loss and fighting it at the same time.* ZORA *gets into position. There's an unsteady calm . . .*]

MARK: . . .

ZORA: . . .

MARK: Backhand.

ZORA: Backhand.

MARK: Two for twenty.

ZORA: Let's go.

MARK: Let's go.

[*They backhand;* ZORA *fucks up.*]

    Again.

ZORA: Again.

[*They backhand through the following dialogue.*]

MARK: Getting good . . . Steady your elbow, / tho.

ZORA: Damnit—

MARK: . . . One more time.

ZORA: One more time.

[*They do it.*]

MARK: Got it?

ZORA: "Got it."

MARK: You got it, next, next, uh, what's, shit, / what's next?

ZORA: Legroom.

MARK: Nah.

ZORA: Yeah, it's Legroom that's next on the list—

MARK: We need three people for that, skip that, skip it, just . . . Ramp It Up.

ZORA: "Ramp it up. / Ramp it up."

MARK: Ten of those, back to back to back.

[*They do a quick exercise of ten reps.*]

MARK: That's ten.

ZORA: Yes, it is.

MARK: How's your shoulder?

ZORA: Fine.

MARK: No it's not, stretch it out.

[ZORA *stretches out.*]

Stop stretching like that.

ZORA: Like what?

MARK: Like that, come on, you're stretching like a back-up dancer, this you, right here—

[*Mocks her.*]

ZORA: No that is not me, / that is you, right there, that is you.

MARK: Paula Abdul stretching mafucker, / right here.

ZORA: That's not / me.

MARK: That's you.

ZORA: I stretch like a normal person.

[*The stretches are totally far from normal now.* MARK *watches.* ZORA *plays it all very seriously.*]

See, like a normal / person—

MARK: *STOP IT* . . . It's like this.

[MARK *goes full-on back-up dancer. He beatboxes as he does it.* ZORA *watches and joins in. It's a routine now.*]

MARK: You good / now.

ZORA: Oh, I'm / good now.

MARK: Nicenicenice. OK. Lesson number—fuck what is it now, like, / lesson number . . .

ZORA: Like ninety, ninety-two or / something—

MARK: Nuh-uh it's like one hundred / and something.

ZORA: Nuh-uh, we were gonna have a party when it got to / a hundred, you said we'd go nuts when we got to a hundred.

MARK: Really? Really? OK—OK, damn, OK, uh— "Lesson ninety-two or something."

ZORA: Hit me.

MARK: All right check it, this one's called "I'm back mafucker."

ZORA: OK yes, / loving that, yes—

MARK: Right, OK, so I'm a demonstrate, k, two moves, knock me down—

ZORA: All right. One—

[Punch.]

And Two, and you're down—

[Trip. He's down . . . and then, slowly, in perfect formation, MARK rises.]

MARK: "I'm back mafucker."

ZORA [applause]: Yes, yes, / yes yes yes! Hahahahahahaa!

MARK: It's not quick, it's not sudden, they gotta think you're down for the count and when you come back you / gotta come back slow, YES.

ZORA: You gotta come / back slow.

MARK: You got it you got it, all right. One—

[*Slight, small hit.*]

ZORA: Uh—

MARK: Uh, what.

ZORA: You're supposed to hit / me.

MARK: I know, that's why I hit / you.

ZORA: Just hit me, come / on and just hit me.

MARK: This is a lesson, not the actual thing, / it's to prepare you for the actual thing.

ZORA: Maaaaaaaaaark . . . Three months. Six days a week. I can take it. Hit me, knock me down, come on, I'm on it.

MARK: —Take a break

ZORA: I don't need / a break.

MARK: Your shoulder is fucked up, OK, / I'm not—

ZORA: Been fucked up, always will be fucked up, I got hit in the side with a sledgehammer by some thief whose ass I beat, fuck that, focus on this, hit me, Mark, hit me.

MARK: . . .

ZORA: You messed up / right now.

MARK: I am messed the fuck up right now.

ZORA: Let me help.
    —I found him.

MARK: . . .

ZORA: One who did it. To Andy. The one who—

Name's Byron.
With the patch on his eye.
Lives not six blocks south.
Not at his house anymore, no, he's lying low now.
Shot a white kid, the one kinda person you don't shoot around here, he's lying low now, he's lying real low.
. . . *No one will miss him.* No one will know.
The only good he will ever do in his entire life is letting himself get wiped clean off so nobody else will ever ever have to feel like—
Worth it.

MARK: Just one guy, that's it.

ZORA: Least we can do.

MARK: No, that's all you.

ZORA: Mark—

MARK: Andy died and we were part of that.
    You were part of that.
    I started that, OK, I admit it, me too, my fault too, I feel sick about it, OK, I don't sleep I don't eat I'm *fucking disgusted*, but you're just ready to jump up, suit up, learn nothing and do something stupid, *don't*, just leave that guy alone, let him go, *it is done*; you do this and you're no better than that guy you're about to cut; no better than those guys who fucked you up on the train 'cause that same crazy they have inside that they can't control? You got that in you too.

ZORA: *Good.*
    If it makes me do what others won't, if it makes me help some-body else, then I'll use it any way every day I will stay lit till everybody else feels what I got in me.
    You got it too, you just think you know how to control it. Don't fight it. *Use it.* 'Cause you can't be good with bad shit, *you gotta meet it*, look at me, *you gotta meet it*, so take all you're holding

back, I need you to pick it all up, I need you to grab it tight and I need you to come with me and use it.

MARK: I get it now.

ZORA: *Yes,* see, yes yes yes, see, / all we need—

MARK: No I get it, I get it, see—
They think we're all just a bunch of animals down here anyway, *you help them* think that. I mean I tried to fight it, tried to bury it, but you just roll around in it don't you, proving all those people right, fight fight fight, there you go, what a good little nigger you are, look at that.
. . . You're about to fuck up your life. More than it already is, more than you know, you're about to end yourself and I am not gonna let you do it, girl. I am not the one.
—I will save your life even if that means I gotta make you hurt for a long long time.
You're not getting off this roof.

ZORA: . . . I gave you a way out.
Because I have *love.*
But you didn't take it and whatever happens next that's on you. Last chance.

MARK: . . . I'm glad Andy's not here to see you right now 'cause he would be so fucking disgusted, God Damn Girl you are pathetic as fuck.

[MARK *pulls out a billy club. It's double sided.* ZORA *has two tasers quick at the ready.*]

ZORA: "Come at me."

[*They run at each other, and they FIGHT. No music, no spectacular stuff, just brutal, tightly choreographed rage. It's desperate, it's long,*

and it's ugly . . . By the end, they are weaponless, swinging at each
other. Nearly shadowboxing. The hits come slower. Slower. Slower.
Exhaustion. Delirious. ZORA *grabs* MARK, *he tries to struggle, she holds*
him. They breathe, spent, sobs . . . They collapse to the ground, the
sound of sirens passing in the distance. Exhausted. Spent. Together.
Calm.]

MARK AND ZORA: . . .

MARK: . . . Got off work last night, saw a—
    saw some mugging.
    Guy grabbed a purse, corner by the Seven-Eleven.
    He runs right at me
    —I let him go past.
    Wanted to see someone else step up.
    Waited to hear someone else say something.
    . . . Nobody said shit.
    Cause *shit never, ever works.*
    This place wants to be hell? *People like living in it, let 'em.*
    Stop sticking your nose in it. Keep your head down. Can't change
    it, too late, you don't like it, then leave.
    Better like that. Feels—
    Feels better than this.

ZORA: . . . That's the final lesson? All that, just, months of that, and
    now—

MARK: Just worry about your own damn self.
    You put your head down. You read a book. Just let it—
    Just *let it.*
    And if you see anything, any goddamn thing . . .

ZORA: "Help nobody but myself". . . Don't need to write it down,
    don't worry. I got it—I know what that is.

MARK: . . . Happy Graduation.

IN THE DARKNESS

JAX: I'm not sure you're as safe as you think.
　　But that comforts you, doesn't it?

[*A montage. As* JAX *speaks, we see* ZORA *and* MARK *in separate pools of light: him on the roof, her exiting to the office.*]

　　I mean if you wanted something changed,
　　if you really wanted it,
　　well, you could change it, right, you could tell your friend, and
　　they could tell their friend, and by the end of it all you've got a
　　lot of people sitting around and they changed something.
　　It'd be easy, right?
　　But you like things the way they are.
　　And that's OK.
　　I mean this city has survived far worse, and look at it,
　　from the skyline it's thriving.
　　Who are you to judge.
　　Stuff on the news? Oh, that's not your Chicago. Not your
　　neighborhood. Not your school, not your family lying in the
　　street, screaming for help, hands up mouth open, that's not Your
　　Chicago.

[JAX *continues, as we see* ZORA *in the office,* MARK *under the stop light,* JAX *in front of the O.M.F.G. sign.*]

> You have one job. So do it.
> Go to work. Go home. Go out. Go to bed.
> Get up in the morning, do it all again,
> you are no one's keeper, you owe nothing, you are not The One.
> Nobody is coming for you, unless you come for them. Until
> they *finally do* come for you. And when they come for you . . .
> nevermind.
> Just do you:
> Just stay safe.

[*We hear the sound of broken, smashed glass. They ignore it . . . Then, finally, a scream. They all look up . . . They stare . . . The music builds, almost triumphant. They know what they have to do.*]